CW01302719

Cover photo: Michelangelo's "Crucifixion," 1492, on display at the Casa Buonarroti in Florence, Italy. Public domain.

Killing God

Christian Fundamentalism and the Rise of Atheism

Rodney Wilson

KILLING GOD: CHRISTIAN FUNDAMENTALISM AND
THE RISE OF ATHEISM © 2015 by Rodney Wilson

All rights reserved.

No part of this book may be used or reproduced in any manner whatsoever without permission except in the case of brief quotations embodied in critical articles and reviews.

ISBN-13: 978-1492165293
ISBN-10: 1492165298

Publishing Note

This project began as a thesis written in 2012 to complete a graduate degree in religion. One bound copy exists, stored away in the school's library, where likely it will never again be seen by human eyes. Prior to being deposited in said library, it was read by only a few individuals other than myself, two of whom are listed in the Acknowledgements.

To give this work a chance to be seen by a few others, I am publishing it. I contacted one *traditional* publisher. An email was exchanged, followed by great silence. I chose, therefore, to bypass the gatekeepers and publish indie-style, via Amazon.com's wildly democratic (anarchic?) CreateSpace.

My primary motivation is that I wish to see the words of the 1,561 anonymous respondents to my online FCNA (Former Christian Now Agnostic/Atheist) survey preserved. Their stories, and that data, make up the second half of this work. It would be shameful on my part to allow their voices to be lost, except in the pages of one dusty bound thesis resting silently among the stacks of an academic library.

Dedication

Dedicated to all women and men of good will who seek the truth, the whole truth, and nothing but the truth—whether it leads to Theism, Atheism, or something in between.

Acknowledgements

The author wishes to thank his thesis director, Professor Harvey Cox of Harvard Divinity School, for his attention and expertise; his thesis advisor, Dean Sue Weaver Schopf of Harvard Extension School, for her guidance; Irán Rodríguez for assistance on technical matters relating to formatting; D.J. Grothe for publicizing the FCNA survey among his cohorts; Klinton Silvey and Trevor Howell for proofreading; Dan Steadman for the final push; and most especially the 1,561 thoughtful respondents to the FCNA survey, without whom this paper would not exist.

Table of Contents

Publishing Note i

Dedication ii

Acknowledgements iii

Abstract vi

Introduction 1

Past is Prelude 13

Killing God: Higher Criticism 23

Killing God: Science 39

Killing God: Conservative Politics 53

Killing God: Earthquakes, Tsunamis and Hellfire 75

Coming Out Atheist 87

Dear John Letters to the Church 95

Conclusion 103

Afterword 113

Appendix I 114

Appendix II 123

Bibliography 267

About the Author 274

List of Figures

Figure 1: The "out of the closet" campaign (ad)........................x

Figure 2: "The Descent of the Modernists" (cartoon).............12

Figure 3: "Have Doubts? So Do We" (ad)...............................22

Figure 4: T-shirt (science v. religion) 38

Figure 5: "All-American Church of the Religious Right".......52

Figure 6: "Damaging Winds" (cartoon)....................................74

Figure 7: T-shirt of the OutCampaign 86

Figure 8: "Blind! Idiot! Rat Fink!" (cartoon)............................94

Figure 9: "God Prefers Kind Atheists" (marquee) 102

Figure 10: Ex-Christian.Net home page 114

Figure 11: Ex-Christian.Net forum..115

Figure 12: Freedom from Religion Foundation home page ..116

Figure 13: Homepage of EvilBible.com 117

Figure 14: Homepage of SkepticsAnnotatedBible.com 118

Figure 15: Homepage of OutCampaign.org 119

Figure 16: OutCampaign Scarlet A (for atheist)....................120

Figure 17: Homepage of The Reason Rally 121

Figure 18: The Friendly Atheist blog 122

Abstract

This study investigates the reasons why some conservative / evangelical / fundamentalist Christians[1] (CEF Christians throughout this text), once true believers, deconvert—that is, reject Christianity and adopt agnosticism/atheism. To determine precisely the motives behind these deconversions, I reviewed spiritual biographies and memoirs of former Christians and conducted an online survey open to *all* agnostics and atheists who were once Christian, which 1,561 respondents completed. Based on my research, I argue that while there are as many factors as there are individuals that collude to dissuade some CEF Christians from belief, primarily there are four: 1) higher criticism of biblical texts, often creating the first cracks in faith's veneer; 2) evolution specifically, which makes a *godless* creation possible, and science generally, which demands naturalistic (not supernatural) rationalism and reasoning, both of which are contrary to a faith-based approach; 3) conservative Christian politics, what I call American Republican Christianity,

---

[1] In this book, *Evangelical Christianity* refers to denominations that emphasize a personal relationship with God, an experience of Jesus as savior (being "born again"), and an accompanying mandate to evangelize in the hope that others might embrace the same faith perspective and be "saved." Rev. Joel Osteen and Franklin Graham are such Christians. *Fundamentalist Christianity* refers to those denominations that are typically both conservative and evangelical *and* firm in propagating the "fundamental" teachings of the faith, particularly in regard to biblical literalism and the inerrancy of scripture. The late Rev. Jerry Falwell was such a Christian.

particularly anti-gay rhetoric, which disillusions Christians of more liberal-progressive leanings; and 4) the inadequacy of various apologetic arguments regarding questions of theodicy and eternal punishing, i.e. traditional hellfire. While some of these causes are more present and more persuasive than others in undermining individual belief in Christian doctrines, the sum total represents an avalanche of opposition to faith that some either cannot or do not wish to outrun. The study concludes that these former CEF Christians represent a growing and often public constituency among agnostics and atheists of the twenty-first century. It is highly likely that their numbers will grow.

"If thou shalt believe in thine heart that God raised Jesus from the dead, thou shalt be saved."

St. Paul, Romans 10:9

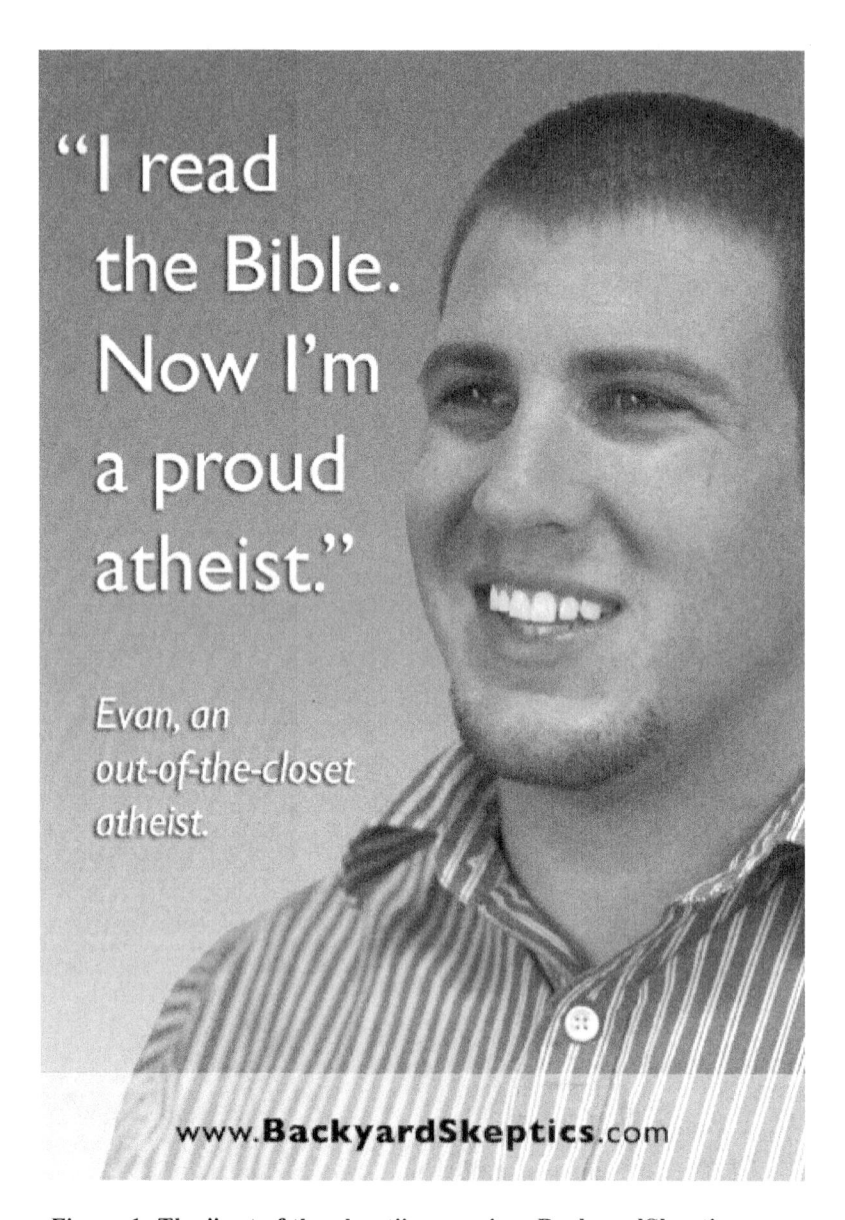

Figure 1: The "out of the closet" campaign, BackyardSkeptics.com. Gray scaled for print. This image is copyright of its owner(s) (if applicable) and is used solely for historical and scholarly illustrative purposes. Used with permission.

Chapter I

Introduction

Hath the fool said in his heart there is no god?[2]

The past two decades have witnessed an avalanche of books, essays, articles, debates, speeches, websites, and bold and provocative advertisements by and about what has been popularly labeled the New Atheism[3] movement, led by the self-described "Four Horsemen,"[4]—evolutionary biologist and former Professor for Public Understanding of Science at Oxford, Richard Dawkins; American philosopher and co-director of the Center for Cognitive Studies at Tufts, Daniel Dennett; widely-published English-American essayist and journalist, the late Christopher Hitchens;[5] and essayist and

---

[2] A play on the familiar passages from Psalm 14:1 and Psalm 53:1 (KJV): "The fool hath said in his heart, there is no God."

[3] *New Atheism* refers to the contemporary movement of atheists/agnostics/skeptics that confronts the faith/belief community with the imperative for a strictly scientific and secular worldview that has overcome all vestiges of supernaturalism and superstition.

[4] So named in the 2-hour videotaped conversation among Dawkins, Dennett, Harris, and Hitchens, released on DVD in 2008 as *Conversations with Richard Dawkins: The Four Horsemen*.

neuroscientist Sam Harris. These four brilliant, articulate, assertive, and charismatic men (and much maligned by some) stand at the forefront of a vocal and outspoken coterie of twenty-first century agnostics and atheists, free thinkers and skeptics, who confront head-on what they perceive to be an endless list of idiosyncrasies and contradictions associated with religious belief. The New Atheists do not blink, they do not cede intellectual or philosophical territory, and they do not concede debate points or grant special privileges to religion, religious belief, or religious individuals. They have evolved a powerful lattice of support networks, public intellectuals (such as the Four Horsemen, and many others), college-based free-thinker groups, podcasts, magazines, and freethinker conferences—all aimed at publicizing their good news: There is no supernatural being to tyrannize us and, therefore, no religious belief should hold the human mind hostage. It is high time, they proclaim by all means available to all who will listen, that religion folds up the revival tent and goes home. God never has been, God is not now, and God never will be. There is nothing to see here.

Truly, these days agnostics and atheists[6] "shout it from the rooftops," as a 2009 *New York Times* page-one headline put it (Goodstein, A1). They advocate vocally and insistently for separation of church (religion) and state (government), for the advance of science and reason, and for an end to any preferred

[5] Christopher Hitchens died in December 2011.

[6] For the purposes of this paper, *agnostic* is defined as one who withholds judgment regarding the existence of the supernatural, but lives as though there is no God; *atheist* is defined as one who categorically denies the existence of the supernatural. Both agnostics and atheists abide by secular (not theological or religious) values and a morality grounded in reason and science, not religion.

or protected status or special privilege for religious persons, religious belief, and religious institutions. New Atheists believe that in regard to this life and this natural world only that which can been observed and tested and quantified and subjected to peer review is worthy of consideration and helpful to human advancement. The rest is diversionary, an impediment to progress, stealing precious time from pursuits that really matter. They also believe that agnostics and atheists must *actively* confront a culture too comfortable with the voices of the religious and especially too accommodating of the demands of politicized religion, often seen, they charge, in national media when a televised platform is given to Pat Robertson, Franklin Graham (famed evangelist Billy Graham's son), Ralph Reed or whoever happens to be the current president of the Southern Baptist Convention, the National Association of Evangelicals, or the Catholic League.

Of course, there have always been agnostics and atheists and freethinking individuals who dissented from the established religious orthodoxy of their age—and were branded with the once (and even now, for many) dreadful names "atheist" or "heretic" as a result. We know that among Golden Age Greeks, five centuries before Christ, debates occurred about the existence of a Being beyond the visible sky—or at least a Being somewhere near Mount Olympus. Myriad examples exist of Europeans who rebelled against the religious officialdom of their days—and some were burned at the stake for spiritual views that were not deemed sufficiently orthodox (literally, of the "correct opinion"). In America, as well, from the days of Pilgrims and Puritans, dissenters (albeit theists) like Roger Williams and Anne Hutchinson spoke up and spoke out, as did a few of our founders of a Deist persuasion and even here and there one or two who denied altogether the existence of A Being Out There.

But something else seems to be occurring these days. Not only are agnostics and atheists bravely vocal and stridently insistent that they deserve a place at the table with everyone else, even if they will not bow their heads when grace is said, within their ranks is also a forceful division of *former conservative-evangelical-fundamentalist Christians* (CEF Christians throughout this text) who have rejected not only the conservatism and/or fundamentalism of their former family of faith, but the idea of belief itself. This growing community of individuals is going public, outing themselves so to speak, and standing four-square against their former denominations, the Christian religion generally, and all theistic philosophies, worldviews, and religious traditions. *We believe in no gods* is their (new) profession of faith, affirmed after discarding their former creeds. And they stand their ground as smart, well-informed *and* biblically-literate ex-Christians—former insiders who have, from their perspective, been deconverted[7] by the liberating light of reason and rationalism that, they prophesy, ultimately will vanquish all vestiges of supernaturalism, religion, and superstition. They are, frankly, quite often far better informed than their erstwhile co-religionists, more intimately familiar with the Bible than most Christians, well-versed in Christian history, Christian doctrine, and with all of

---

[7] *Deconversion* refers to the process whereby former Christian converts have renounced faith (deconverted) in the supernatural and in religion, often a long and difficult process, occasionally even marked ritually with a somewhat facetious "reverse baptism."

the arguments for and against belief in God and for and against belief in their former savior, Jesus. Because they once held so tightly and sincerely and loyally to the beliefs they once held so dear and now utterly reject, they present a formidable opponent in modern-day Mars Hill[8] debates. They did not reject their former faith without first examining it, in many cases far more closely than most will ever do.

A growing number of former CEF Christians have lately "come out"[9] and proclaimed their religious orientation—whether as non-believer, agnostic, atheist, skeptic, freethinker, or secular humanist. For some of these former Christians (especially in the initial period after deconversion), the need to spread the gospel of deconversion and the *objective reasonableness* of atheism is as urgent as was their former need to publish the gospel of Christian conversion and the peace they once found in communion with Jesus. In the Internet age, rife with websites devoted to self-described freethinkers, to agnosticism and atheism—atheists.org, atheists-online.com, 4atheists.com, gods4suckers.net, atheistnation.net, exchristians.net (see Figures 10 and 11), and many others—one can encounter groups and forums and posts by former CEF Christians who no longer believe in the Christian faith or in any form of supernaturalism; and having once been on the inside of these organizations, they are adroit in pointing out inconsistencies in doctrine, lifestyle, biblical texts, and belief.

---

[8] A reference to St. Paul's famous debate on Mars Hill, Athens, in Acts 17.

[9] The "coming out" terminology is used quite frequently by these groups and likened often to the gay rights movement's insistence that gay people "come out of the closet" in order to effect change.

Several former Christians have recently published memoirs documenting their deconversion process, including former evangelical journalist and religion reporter William Lobdell (*Losing My Religion: How I Lost My Faith Reporting on Religion in America—and Found Unexpected Peace*, 2009); former Christian apologist John Loftus (*Why I Became an Atheist: A Former Preacher Rejects Christianity*[10], 2008); former evangelical, now self-described freethinker, Betty Brogaard (*The Homemade Atheist: A Former Evangelical Woman's Freethought Journey to Happiness*, 2010); former Bible translator and missionary to a small tribe of Amazonian Indians, Daniel Everett (*Don't Sleep, There are Snakes: Life and Language in the Amazonian Jungle*, 2008); former fundamentalist Edward T. Babinski (author of *Leaving the Fold: Testimonies of Former Fundamentalists*, 2003); and Freedom From Religion Foundation[11] (see Figure 12) co-president and self-described "friendly neighborhood atheist," the former evangelist Dan Barker (*Godless: How an Evangelical Preacher Became One of America's Leading Atheists*, 2008).

---

[10] The opening refrain of Loftus's introduction indicates that this former Christian apologist is an apologist still, only now for "the other side": "This book . . . is specifically written to devout Christians by a former Christian minister and apologist for their faith who is now an atheist. It is also written for Christians who are questioning their faith, as well as for skeptics who want to learn how to effectively argue against Christianity" (11).

[11] The Freedom from Religion Foundation (FFRF) is among the nation's leading secular advocates for separation of church and state. FFRF is responsible for many of the pro-separation billboards and lawsuits against governments for perceived violation of the First Amendment's Establishment Clause.

Other well-known and leading voices of the skeptical/atheist movement are also former CEF Christians, including former fundamentalist and Moody Bible Institute-trained Bible scholar Bert Ehrman (author of *Misquoting Jesus: The Story Behind Who Changed the Bible and Why*; *Jesus Interrupted: Revealing the Hidden Contradictions in the Bible (And Why We Don't Know About Them)*; *Lost Christianities: The Battle for Scripture and the Faiths We Never Knew*; *Lost Scriptures: The Battle for Scripture and the Faiths We Never Knew*; and *God's Problem: How the Bible Fails to Answer Our Most Important Question—Why We Suffer*); former Baptist preacher and professor of theology Robert Price (*Incredible Shrinking Son of Man: How Reliable Is the Gospel Tradition?*; *Jesus is Dead*; and *Inerrant the Wind: The Evangelical Crisis in Biblical Authority*); founder of the Skeptics Society and publisher of *Skeptic* magazine Michael Shermer; and former voice of the "Point of Inquiry" podcast of the Center for Inquiry (advocacy group for "a secular society based on science, reason, freedom of inquiry, and humanist values"[12]) and now president of the James Randi Education Foundation, D. J. Grothe.

From each of these individuals and from the vast array of "testimonies" of other ex-CEF Christians, including the 1,591 who responded in early February 2012 to an extensive online survey (Former Christian Now Agnostic/Atheist Survey, FCNA throughout this text) about their journey to non-belief, one is able to pull together the varied reasons a CEF Christian might commence *and* conclude a journey along the path less

---

[12] From the official Website of the Center for Inquiry, accessed on April 22, 2010, at www.centerforinquiry.net.

taken, the one that leads to a godless universe. The words and experiences of CEF Christians, therefore, will provide a foundational structure upon which the thesis of this work will be supported—words such as these by Charles Templeton (1915-2001), a former born-again Christian and close friend of and fellow evangelist with America's most well-known preacher, the Rev. Billy Graham:

> Surely it is a negation of human experience and intellectual and scientific progress to cling to the archaic and untenable notion that the universe and our lives are the creation of and in the control of a primitive tribal deity, a male chauvinist much given to anger, intolerance, and fits of pique when crossed. (Templeton 43)

I must acknowledge that the testimony of the disgruntled is often viewed with some suspicion, and rightly so. Perhaps the aggrieved have an axe to grind, a viewpoint to evangelize, even a battle to win. I am not unaware of this possibility. I believe still, however, that the experiences of former CEF Christians, told as they tell them in their own words, offer significant insight into why they let go of God and how they understand that process.

This thesis, using in part first-person testimony, will investigate specifically the reasons given by former CEF Christians to explain why they now reject the faith experience and why they left not only their former denominations but the Christian faith altogether; and, in exchange, adopted agnosticism or atheism, thereby embracing a godless and stridently secular worldview where science and reason and rationalism, not "Thy Word,"[13] are the lights unto their paths.

The primary question to be addressed in this undertaking is this: What role did the church itself *and* fundamentalist doctrines and conservative politics play in the loss of faith? Among the subordinate questions to be studied are these: What is the origin of the change of mind? What happened to continue the process that led to the renunciation of belief? How difficult and how long was this process? Were there moments of fear and anxiety? How did their families of faith/spirit and of DNA/flesh respond to the rejection of shared cherished values? Is there anger over lost years in the church? Why do many former Christians become *evangelical* (some make the charge, even fundamentalist) about their non-belief? Are there moments in which one doubts the new doubt and wonders if, in fact, there may be a supernatural? How do CEF Christians, especially those in leadership, respond to individuals who have rejected their faith and spiritual disciplines? How differently does one live his/her life as an atheist, compared to how he or she lived when a CEF Christian? Could anything have preserved their faith? Could anything restore it? These questions and more will be addressed in the words of former Christians themselves, gleaned from memoirs and the FCNA Survey.

I will argue that four primary characteristics of CEF Christianity actually work *against* the perseverance of belief in these systems and, ironically, greatly contribute in our scientific and pluralistic world to a growing number who are unable to maintain trust and belief in CEF Christianity or in any religion. I will also argue that CEF Christianity has four

---

[13] Psalm 119:105 (KJV): "Thy Word is a lamp unto my feet and a light unto my path."

tendencies that are, for many, killing God. These are: 1) rigid, unyielding belief in biblical inerrancy; 2) rejection of the supremacy of the scientific method for discerning truth about the natural world, including rejection of evolution as the only scientific story of origins; 3) conservative politics and its harsh condemnation of those who challenge their political and social orthodoxies, such as homosexuals; and 4) unsatisfactory answers to the question of pain and suffering (theodicy) and doctrines about eternal punishment in hellfire.

In addition, I will show that the faith-to-no-faith process is generally a difficult one that begins in trepidation and even fear and anxiety, and sometimes leads to anger at perceived "lost years" during the faith journey and anger at the God and belief system that once were held so dear and sacred, culminating finally in an acceptance of a good life without a god or the supernatural, with a sense of contentedness and psychological freedom. But first, some historical perspective.

In fact, the whole machinery of our intelligence, our general ideas and laws, fixed and external objects, principles, persons, and gods, are so many symbolic, algebraic expressions. They stand for experience; experience which we are incapable of retaining and surveying in its multitudinous immediacy. We should flounder hopelessly, like the animals, did we not keep ourselves afloat and direct our course by these intellectual devices. Theory helps us to bear our ignorance of fact.

George Santayana, *The Sense of Beauty*, 1896

Figure 2: "The Descent of the Modernists," E.J. Pace, first appeared in William Jennings Bryan fundamentalist apologetic, *Seven Questions in Dispute* (New York: Fleming H. Revell Company, 1924) 2. This image is copyright of its owner(s) (if applicable) and is used solely for historical and scholarly illustrative purposes.

Chapter II

Past is Prelude

To say that atheism is credible is to suggest that the atheist may be right; to say that the atheist may be right is to suggest that the Christian may be wrong; to say that the Christian may be wrong is to suggest that faith may be an unreliable guide to knowledge; to say that faith may be an unreliable guide to knowledge is to suggest that each and every tenet of Christianity should be reexamined in the light of reason—and from here all hell breaks loose as the process of deconversion rushes headlong to its logical destination.
  —George H. Smith, former Christian, *Why Atheism?* (17, 18)

Naming the contemporary movement of an organized band of smart, outspoken non-believers the *New Atheism* is an acknowledgment that the propositions themselves represent little that is actually new: there is no god, the Bible is a human document, and science is humanity's most dependable method for discerning truth and creating the conditions requisite for the good life. While the propagation tools of the New Atheists are cutting edge (Internet being primary), views similar to theirs have been advocated by certain individuals and classes, albeit always a small minority, for the entirety of human history.

Among Classical Greeks and ancient Romans were great minds, usually the elite, who openly pondered the question of the existence of the gods; and some who outright denied the supernatural. In the East, religio-philosophies like Buddhism and Confucianism originally either denied or simply found the matter of gods an unimportant consideration that followed (if at all) far behind the existential goals of enlightenment and proper internal and external relationships. In the West, the ages of Renaissance, Reformation, Reason, Enlightenment and Science offered alternative answers, non-supernatural, to the fundamental questions of existence and gave rise to an abiding Western skepticism, rationalism, secularism, and for some, agnosticism.

While founded in part by men and women who wanted to spread the Christian religion, the founders of the United States did not represent a monolithic assemblage of "true" Christians, as some CEF Christians today would have us believe, but a diversity of spiritual lifestyles, primarily mainline Christian and Deist. While most of the nation's original architects acknowledged Providence and/or a Supreme Judge—both names for a divinity appear in the American Declaration of Independence, for example—they were generally more educated than and less traditionally religious than the average American.

In America, the First and Second Great Awakenings (the former, pre-Independence, and the latter, pre-Civil War) emboldened the faith of the American people and gave way among many to great periods of intense Christian religious devotion. The Second Great Awakening, for example, left behind "burned-over districts" (especially in Western and

Upstate New York) where every Christian denomination under the sun came calling for converts and where religious fervor gave birth to millennial movements and new denominations—e.g., Christian Science, Bible Students (later, Jehovah's Witnesses) and Mormonism. But behind the revival curtain there were also skeptics and freethinkers, few in number, but fervent in their views and intellectually vigorous in the defense thereof, capable of creating waves across the intellectual world. Robert Green Ingersoll (1833-1899) comes quickly to mind (more about him later).

Before World War II, most CEF Christians who experienced a falling out with their faith simply packed up and moved gingerly along the spectrum of *theism*, settling at liberal Christian or Deism; few chucked it all for agnosticism or atheism. There is little data on such ones prior to the midpoint of the twentieth century.

A 2008 study by Harvard professor David Hempton, published as *Evangelical Disenchantment: Nine Portraits of Faith and Doubt*, examines the spiritual lives of nine well-known individuals of cultural distinction in the 19th- and early-20th centuries who once wholeheartedly cast their lots with evangelical Christianity only to cut the cord as they matured intellectually and, they would surely say, spiritually. These European and American men and women—by birth year, Sarah Grimké (1792-1873), Theodore Dwight Weld (1803-1895), Francis W. Newman (1805-1897), Elizabeth Cady Stanton (1815-1902), George Eliot (1819-1880), Francis Willard (1839-1898), Vincent Van Gogh (1853-1890), Edmund Gosse (1849-1928), and James Baldwin (1924-1997)—each gave witness to a sincere and strong evangelical experience. In evangelical parlance, they had been "saved" or "born again" in accord with John 3 and had conformed their lives and thoughts and behaviors accordingly—and they all eventually experienced a great *disenchantment* (thus Hempton's title) and severed their ties with evangelical Christianity.

Many shared themes emerge between this small group in Hempton's study and former CEF Christians a century later: rejection of the inerrancy of scripture is universal;[14] resistance against a sense of mental confinement within the restraint of doctrine; weariness with end-times prophecy (apocalyptic preachers William Miller and John Nelson Darby had disciples among these nine); moral failures of evangelical leadership;[15] the advance of science; dissatisfaction with theologies of theodicy and doctrines about hellfire; and disappointment at the failure of evangelicals to take strong moral stands—in the case of the nineteenth century, *against* slavery and *for* women's suffrage; in the case of the twentieth century, *against* Jim Crow segregation and *for* minority rights, including, as we will see, gay rights.

Prior to the advent of the scientific method and the twentieth century's unrelenting emphasis on science as the only trustworthy means of acquiring knowledge, naturally there existed more unanswerable queries about the universe and the origin of life and, therefore, more gaps for the god hypothesis to govern the question and provide an answer. In the second

---

[14] For Elizabeth Cady Stanton, "the Bible was patriarchal through and through" (Hempton 112).

[15] "His [Theodore Dwight Weld] good friend, Russell Judd, minister of the Free Church in Brooklyn, was accused of sexual abuse of ten young girls" (Hempton 82).

decade of the twenty-first century, however, it is easily possible for moderns to live fully integrated intellectual and spiritual lives *without* religion, certainly without religion in the traditional sense, and to live a good life *without* God. This luxury, if it is such, generally did not exist prior to the twentieth century.

It is crucial to note, therefore, that while Hempton's subjects and others like them may have journeyed far from their former fold, they did not, at least publicly, choose agnosticism or atheism. They did not outright reject the concept of God—only the understanding of the Divine as codified by their former denominations. Therefore, these primarily nineteenth-century "backsliders" found themselves drawn not to agnosticism but to more liberal or deistic traditions. As Hempton writes, "Sarah Grimké, in common with many other women who were active in the cause of antislavery and women's rights, did not become atheists or secularists. They simply reconstructed their spiritual lives without the aid of formal religious authorities and institutions" (98). Vincent van Gogh likewise did not (in van Gogh's view, at least) abandon God. While he did proclaim the "God of the clergymen" to be "as dead as a doornail," and the clergymen in turn considered van Gogh an "atheist," van Gogh himself maintained faith in "love": "Now call it God, or human nature or whatever you like," van Gogh wrote, "but there is something which I cannot define in a system though it is very much alive and very real, and [I] see that as God, or just as good as God" (Hempton 129). Van Gogh, according to Hempton, would not "have appropriated descriptive labels such as atheism, agnosticism, or infidelity for this new faith, for it was based not on rationality, but on sense and experience, on impressions and expressions" (130).

The fear of atheism, however, *was* part of the religious discussion of the second half of the nineteenth century, the time during which van Gogh and Sarah Grimké and most of the others in Hempton's book lived. Take John Bascom (1827-1911). He was a graduate of Andover Theological Seminary (1855) and in middle-age served as president of the University of Wisconsin. While president of the university, in 1881, he wrote an essay for *The North American Review* titled "Atheism in Colleges." Bascom feared that European skepticism would soon overtake England and then America: "How far is this unbelief finding its way into American colleges?" (32), he asked. Unfortunately, in his view, the "evil of unbelief" (36) was already lapping at America's shores. Science, Boscom charged, was "the one great intellectual movement of our age" that had been brought "into the service of unbelief" (33). Only strong and consistent leadership in American colleges could properly "defend our young men from unbelief" (40).

Then came the Great War (1914-1918), Albert Einstein's non-personal "god," Sigmund Freud's God-as-exalted-father psychoanalysis, the triumph of science, and widespread dissemination and understanding of Darwin's theory of evolution, especially leading up to and following the Dayton, Tennessee, (so-called) Scopes Monkey Trial[16] of 1925. The tide Bascom feared and wrote about in 1881, bolstered by science, was waxing, especially in American higher education.

---

[16] Properly known as *The State of Tennessee v. John Thomas Scopes*.

Sixty years after Bascom's warning to American colleges, and twenty-five years after the Scopes Trial, the French Catholic philosopher Jacques Maritain in 1949 addressed the University of Notre Dame on the meaning of contemporary atheism (later published in *The Review of Politics*). Maritain warned against a "thunderous bursting forth" of atheistic philosophy, a culmination of three centuries of what he called "progressive degradation of the idea of God" introduced by "bourgeois rationalism" (269) and the failure of the church to "lead in the protest of the poor and of the movement of labor," largely ceding these noble causes, Maritain charged, to the secular and the atheistic (277). It was the abandonment of "practical" Christianity (a form of Social Gospel) and the church's abandonment of "the immense herd of the hopeless" that had in large part nourished the rise of contemporary atheism, he asserted (277).

And that seemed to be that. There was no turning back, no way to reclaim for Christ the marketplace of ideas. Over the next decade, godless Christianity and Christian atheism (embracing the ethics of Jesus sans the supernaturalism) emerged among some American professors of theology and religion as the only viable way to salvage the ethical and moral mandates of the Christian religion. In 1965, theologian Harvey Cox tapped into the deep-seated human need for secure footing, this time in the brave new world of secular modernity. In *The Secular City: A Celebration of Its Liberties and an Invitation to Its Discipline*, which ultimately sold one million copies, Cox argued not that God was dead, but that the times had changed and that theology must change as well. He sought to build a theological bridge that would connect the religious with secular urbanity. The following year, *Time* magazine grabbed the nation's attention with a provocative Easter season cover story. Against a black background, the editors of *Time* asked their readers a stark question (in blood-red letters that in many King James Bibles highlight the words of Jesus): "Is God Dead?" According to *Time*, a "small band of radical theologians" were arguing that God was dead and that the churches had to learn to "get along well without him." Christianity needed to "write a theology without *theos*," according to these radical new theologians. These Christian atheists were ready to move on, from a theism-based Christianity to one that was non-theistic. Science and urbanization, along with mechanization and modernity, had changed the world. A personal God was no longer required.

The obituaries, however, were premature. While in the mid-1960s many historians, sociologists, and theologians believed that secularism was the next big thing and that religion would take a seat in the last row of the bus, no longer occupying a position in "the public life of the secular metropolis" (Cox, *Secular* 2), the spirit of the age (for believers, the "s" would be capitalized) intervened and gave birth to revival, to Hal Lindsay, to Rapture speculation, to Jerry Falwell and the Moral Majority, to Jim and Tammy-style televangelism, to Reagan Democrats and the Christian Coalition, to the "tsunami of Pentecostalism" (Cox, *Future* 197) and the mainstreaming thereof (think: former Attorney General John Ashcroft), and to Pentecostalism's more modern sibling, the charismatic movement that crossed all denominational lines, bringing a breath of fresh air to American Christianity.

It is against this *New* Christianity that the *New* Atheism sets itself in opposition. The disenchanted evangelicals of the nineteenth century did not abandon the hope of God altogether. Van Gogh, Stanton, and Weld were disillusioned, but they still believed in *something*. In the twentieth century, the age of unbelief gained ground. Defensive (and offensive) measures were taken—fundamentalism and post-Vietnam and post-Watergate revival—but for many, science and secularism remained the only way out.

The twenty-first century offers more opportunity than any previous age to comfortably *and* quickly slide (downward or upward, depending on perspective) along the spectrum of theism to atheism. Science now offers a fulfilling explanation for most of the traditional religion-generating mysteries: how did we get here?; where did the world come from?; why are there tornadoes and earthquakes? While even today, most disenchanted CEF Christians generally remain Christian, of the mainstream or liberal variety, the disenchanted ones are more likely in 2012 than they were in 1812 or 1912 to take the final step down modernity's staircase, landing at atheism. To that story we now turn.

Figure 3: "Have Doubts? So Do We," BackyardSkeptics.com. (Gray scaled for print.) This image is copyright of its owner(s) (if applicable) and is used solely for historical and scholarly illustrative purposes. Used with permission.

Chapter III

Killing God: Higher Criticism

There was a gradual transition from believing [the Bible] was the infallible word of god, to believing it was divinely inspired, to eventually discovering it was nothing but myth and legend.
—R1521, 18-29, male[17]

Bart Ehrman (b. 1955) was a true believer. Although raised a "socializing Episcopalian" (*Misquoting* 4) in Kansas, shortly after beginning to attend Campus Life Youth for Christ events, the fifteen-year-old accepted Christ as his personal savior and was "born again." At lightning speed, Ehrman committed himself to regular Bible study, hoping to literally obey Paul's words to another young man in the faith, Timothy: "Study to shew thyself approved unto God, a workman that needeth not to be ashamed, rightly dividing the word of truth" (2 Tim. 2.15, KJV).

Upon completing high school in 1973, Ehrman enrolled at Chicago's Moody Bible Institute, majoring in Bible theology, studying beneath professors who had, as a condition of employment, pledged that they were fundamentalist in outlook

---

[17] Respondents to the FCNA Survey are referenced in this paper by Response Number (in this case, R1521), by age category, and by sex.

and that they would teach the faith from a fundamentalist perspective.[18] After completing the three-year Moody diploma, Ehrman transferred to Wheaton College, also near Chicago, but a bit less conservative than Moody's enterprise and the alma mater of Billy Graham. At Wheaton, he majored in English literature and studied biblical Greek. In short order, he began confronting surprising and discomforting facts, such as what appeared to be contradictions in the New Testament text and the non-existence of autographs (originals) of the Greek scriptures. Troubled by the absence of original manuscripts of the New Testament and the dependence for translation, therefore, on copies of copies of copies, Ehrman begin a deep and scholarly (*and* spiritual) study of the Greek texts.

Graduating from Wheaton, he gained admittance to graduate school at Princeton Theological Seminary, where he studied under one of the world's leading experts on New Testament textual criticism. The more Ehrman learned of biblical exegesis, the less convinced he became about inerrancy of the Bible and, consequently, the more unsettled he found himself and his relationship to his conservative church. After his second semester at Princeton, he recalls, "the floodgates opened" (Ehrman, *Misquoting* 9); forever after, his understanding of scripture's reliability and authority was altered: "[M]y study of the Greek New Testament, and my investigations into the manuscripts that contain it, led to a radical rethinking of my understanding of what the Bible is" (11). Not too many semesters later, the former born-again fundamentalist Christian had altogether rejected belief in the

---

[18] All biographical facts about Ehrman are from his book *Misquoting Jesus: The Story Behind Who Changed the Bible and Why*.

supernatural origin of the Bible and replaced that doctrine with the view that the Bible is "a human book from beginning to end" (11). He writes:

> It is a radical shift from reading the Bible as an inerrant blueprint for our faith, life and future, to seeing it as a very human book, with very human points of view, many of which differ from one another and none of which provides the inerrant guide to how we should live. This is the shift in my own thinking that I ended up making, and to which I am now [writing in 2005] fully committed. (13)

Professor Ehrman was not the first CEF Christian (and most certainly will not be the last) to begin the descent (or ascent, depending on one's perspective) to non-belief in the wake of the recognition that the Bible is not, literally speaking, the Word of God, and that the Bible is not an inerrant "rule of faith and conduct" (as many CEF membership creeds put it). The fundamentalist/conservative doctrine of verbal-plenary inspiration of the Bible, the idea that the text as originally written is without error or contradiction, has left many on the shores of unbelief. When a Christian accepts the doctrine of inerrancy of scripture, contrary evidence—of which there *is* plenty—creates cognitive dissonance and raises troubling spiritual questions. For those unable to satisfactorily amend their belief about the Bible, biblical agnosticism emerges, followed by agnosticism about one's religion, and, finally, agnosticism about the existence of any type of supernatural world. That is the story of Bart Ehrman and the former Christians in this study.

Another variant on this pattern is journalist William Lobdell, author of *Losing My Religion: How I Lost My Faith Reporting on Religion in America—and Found Unexpected Peace*. Once upon a time, Lobdell believed in an interventionist Christian God revealed in Christ and unerringly attested to in the Bible. Acquiring his dream job as religion reporter for the *Los Angeles Times* was, Lobdell then believed, sure and certain evidence that "God had answered my prayers more completely than I could have ever imagined" (60). During the first year at the newspaper, Lobdell wrote 145 stories, a feat he chalked up to "the subtle hand of the Lord at work. Another God thing" (61). Within a decade, however, Lobdell had stopped believing in any type of god or supernatural, rejecting all theistic philosophies. Lobdell's deconversion, from evangelical Christian to atheist, was slow and painful. His loss of faith, however, did not begin specifically with questions about the inerrancy of scripture (those came quickly later) as it had for Ehrman, but in the midst of investigating and reporting on the Roman Catholic clergy sex abuse investigation:

> . . . it now appears to me [he is writing in 2009] as a Road to Damascus moment that I kept safely locked away in my subconscious. . . . I had written so much about the redemptive power of faith, but I had never seen, in a real and personal way, the opposite: the damage religions could do in the hands of bad people. . . . This short supply of holiness was something that began to stick in my throat, a disconcerting fact that I washed down with prayer and Christian aphorisms such as "Don't mix up man's shortcomings with God." (104-05)

The fatal blow to Lobdell's belief, however, *was* delivered by his gnawing doubt about the reliability of scripture. As he covered stories involving members of other faiths and of the Church of Jesus Christ of Latter-day Saints (Mormons), for example, he began to become embarrassingly conscious of strong parallels between the psychology of Mormon belief in the Book of Mormon and Mormon defense of that text (even in the face of what many claim are glaring inconsistencies and DNA evidence that contradicts Book of Mormon claims about Native Americans) and CEF Christian beliefs about the Bible and their ardent defense of the inerrancy of that sacred text (at least, in the original manuscripts). *Why am I able to doubt the Book of Mormon or the Qur'an*, he asked himself, but unable to doubt the Bible? Why the double standard?

Further pondering on this question convinced Lobdell that his belief in an inerrant Bible had nothing whatsoever to do with the historicity or credibility of the book itself, or with scientific investigation, but with happenstance: he "just happened to grow up with the stories of the Bible." He was, naturally therefore, "more used to" the supernatural claims of the virgin birth and miracles of Jesus and resurrection of the dead than he was with the supernatural claims of other faiths (126-27). The acceptance of certain religious claims—*his* religion's claims—on the basis that he was accustomed to them began to feel as intellectually unreasonable to him as the unquestioned acceptance that adherents of other religions placed in their holy books and doctrines. Lobdell had no choice—he had to let go of biblical inerrancy. That loss, coupled with covering the corrupt underside of religion, were the two pressing factors that account for why this former self-proclaimed evangelical Christian is now a self-proclaimed agnostic.

The New Atheists and certainly the former CEF Christians of the movement know that losing faith in the inerrancy of scripture sometimes leads to losing faith *in belief itself*. Many agnostics and atheists, therefore, turn their energies toward debunking the Bible and the supernatural claims that are made about it. They know that belief in the Bible *must* be shaken before a person is able to admit doubts about belief in the supernatural. Websites such as EvilBible.com and SkepticsAnnotatedBible.com are designed, according to EvilBible.com, to "spread the vicious truth about the Bible" (see Figures 13 and 14). Debunking the Bible, of course, is a tried and true method of gaining deconverts and skeptics.

The technique goes way back. The most famous atheist of nineteenth-century America was an expert with it. The Great Agnostic (as many called him) Robert Green Ingersoll (1833-1899) engaged in unrelenting blistering attacks against all forms of religious belief, specifically challenging the Bible and the Christian religion. He delivered scores of vitriolic speeches all over America excoriating the Bible and lambasting religious faith. Near the end of his life, he delivered a speech titled "About the Holy Bible"[19] (1894), a summation of his thoughts about what most of his fellow citizens called the Good Book. It is a scathing critique of the Bible that would make today's "Great Agnostic" Richard Dawkins or the late Christopher Hitchens very proud.

---

[19] All quotes in the next two paragraphs are from Ingersoll's 1894 speech "About the Holy Bible," unnumbered pages, http://manybooks.net/titles/ingersolother08About_the_Holy_Bible.html, accessed October 21, 2009.

The Bible, Ingersoll charged, originated with "a few ignorant, impoverished" tribes; it is "filled with mistakes and contradictions"; it is "the enemy of intellectual freedom"; and it "imprisons the brain and corrupts the heart." The Bible is "savagery, not philosophy"; it is "the enemy of art" (by forbidding "graven images"); it was written by "savages" who believed in "slavery, polygamy and wars of extermination." Never one to shrink from the mission of destroying belief in the Bible, Ingersoll in this essay provided a brief scorched-earth commentary on many of the books of the Bible: Ezra is "of no importance, of no use"; Nehemiah has "not a word…worth reading"; Daniel "is a disordered dream, a nightmare"; Lamentations "is simply a continuance of the ravings of the same insane pessimist" who wrote Jeremiah. He writes of the "mistranslations," "interpolations," and "contradictions" of the four Gospels; the "absurdities" of the miracle stories about Jesus; and he goes so far as to hurl a direct attack against Jesus himself, usually a sacrosanct personage, referencing many of the most-loved words of Jesus ("love your enemies" and "turn the other cheek," for example) and tearing them apart, declaring them rubbish, and proclaiming that "only the insane could give or follow this advice." Yes, the Great Agnostic called Jesus insane. (No need to wonder why there was a fundamentalist counter-attack in the first decades of the twentieth century!)

Ingersoll concluded his war on the Bible with a full-throated assault. It is a long diatribe, intense, no holds-barred, still widely circulated today on many agnostic/atheist websites and, therefore, even now relevant if we are to understand the ferocity with which some today attack the Bible, as a weapon in the battle against what they believe is the danger of fundamentalist Christianity:

> This book is the enemy of freedom, the support of slavery. This book sowed the seeds of hatred in families and nations, fed the flames of war, and impoverished the world. This book is the breastwork of kings and tyrants—the enslaver of women and children. This book has corrupted parliaments and courts. This book has made colleges and universities the teachers of error and the haters of science. This book has filled Christendom with hateful, cruel, ignorant and warring sects. This book taught men to kill their fellows for religion's sake. This book founded the Inquisition, invented the instruments of torture, built the dungeons in which the good and loving languished, forged the chains that rusted in their flesh, erected the scaffolds whereon they died. This book piled fagots about the feet of the just. This book drove reason from the minds of millions and filled the asylums with the insane. This book has caused fathers and mothers to shed the blood of their babes. This book was the auction block on which the slave-mother stood when she was sold from her child. This book filled the sails of the slave-trader and made merchandise of human flesh. This book lighted the fires that burned "witches" and "wizards." This book filled the darkness with ghouls and ghosts, and the bodies of men and women with devils. This book polluted the souls of men with the infamous dogma of eternal pain. This book made credulity the greatest of virtues, and investigation the greatest of crimes. This book filled nations with hermits, monks and nuns—with the pious and the useless. This book placed the ignorant and unclean saint above the philosopher and philanthropist. This book taught man to despise the joys of this life, that he might be happy in another—to waste this world for the sake of the next. I attack this book because it is the enemy of human

liberty—the greatest obstruction across the highway of human progress. Let me ask the ministers one question: How can you be wicked enough to defend this book? (Ingersoll, "About the Holy Bible" n.p.)

Clearly, Ingersoll is overstating it a bit. He's angry and, it could be argued, even a bit hateful. But his views of 120 years ago remain those of many within today's agnostic/atheist community, such as the producers of Infidels.org and PositiveAtheism.org, where Ingersoll's thunderous denunciation of the Bible can be found, one under a headline referencing "Ingersoll the Magnificent."

In reviewing the data from the FCNA Survey (see Questions 12, 13, 15), the loss of belief in the absolute veracity of the Bible was a significant contributing factor in the rejection of the Christian faith. Slightly over fifty percent (51.4%) of non-CEF respondents indicated that being exposed to higher criticism and non-fundamentalist interpretations of the Bible played a "very important" or "somewhat important" role in their deconversion. For former CEF Christians, the significance was slightly more, with 54.5% indicating that these things were "very important" or "somewhat important" in their deconversion process. While 72.2% of former non-CEF Christians believed, prior to deconversion, that the Bible was either "the infallible, inerrant Word of God" or the "Word of God, written by men under divine inspiration," 97.0% of former CEF Christians believed such. Post-deconversion, about half of each group believes that the Bible remains "a significant cultural document" but that it is "by no means of supernatural / divine origin"; and about half feel the Bible is "no more special than any other book of antiquity." Former CEF Christians are slightly more likely to grant the Bible a slightly higher consideration ("significant cultural document"), 55.2% versus 53.1%.

No other issue in the FCNA Survey elicited as much input as the open-ended question on the role of loss of belief in Bible inerrancy on the deconversion process of the respondents—330 of 391 (84.4%) of former CEF Christians responded (see Question 14), some with paragraphs of commentary, for a total of 55 pages of single-spaced, 12-point text! No other question fueled as extensive an outpouring of thoughts, which is indicative of the primary importance of rejection of biblical inerrancy in the deconversion process.

The experiences described by survey respondents, especially former CEF Christians, were quite similar to one another. They had been raised to believe that the Bible is perfect, error-free, the divine Word of God, the only source of written communication from God, and the final arbiter of truth in all matters. The respondents, when they were Christian, generally were content with the doctrine of scriptural inerrancy and relied on the Bible as their sole guide along their church's narrow path to righteousness and peace with God. But then something happened. The insupportable doctrine of biblical inerrancy was found wanting. "It started with small questions/observations," such as the two genealogies of Jesus in the Gospels, wrote R1411 (30-39, male). All attempts to reconcile these small differences that might not even bother adherents of a non-inerrancy background proved fruitless. Persistent and reinforced doubts about the doctrine of an inerrant text led to more doubt about the trustworthiness of the Bible as a source of revelatory truth about God. Like many others, R1405 (50-59, male) made every effort to reconcile his belief in inerrancy with what appeared to be contradictions of such, all to no avail: "I believed the Bible could be shown to be factually correct. My attempts to demonstrate that led me to discover the many errors in it."

Much like Bart Ehrman and John Loftus, a seed of doubt—or from their perspective, a seed of truth—took root in their thinking. As that seed germinated, many of these respondents slowly (in a few cases, rapidly) lost confidence in the Bible as a perfect source of divine revelation. Some experienced guilt, psychological trauma, and even spiritual terror when the (biblical) rug was pulled from beneath them. Writes participant R1558 (50-59, male):

> My deconversion lasted over a period of about seven years. It was very, very difficult, especially the first stages because the "sin" of questioning my beliefs and the Bible was a nearly insurmountable obstacle. Ultimately I concluded that the Old Testament was the mythology of an ancient people, and the New Testament was the literature of an emerging cult, shaped in part by internal conflicts, agendas, infighting, and corruption.

Another respondent (R1368, 30-39, male) wrote that his close study of the Bible, a book he once believed to be inerrant, began out of "genuine interest" and a desire to get "something more" out of his faith. Instead of encountering a mesmerizing and obviously other-worldly book, however, it became for him "impossible . . . to believe." In short order, he "progressed from Biblical literalism to a more liberal interpretation," and then "settled in to viewing the Bible as mostly erroneous and largely immoral." The deconversion process took "several years." Recalling the process, this respondent suggests that loss of belief in the integrity of the Bible and "the conflict between Evangelic Christianity and modern science (biology and physics in particular)" as well as "the various social conflicts (bigotry towards homosexuals) provided [the] catalyst" for his complete denunciation of the Christian faith.

In accord with evangelical "advertising" oversell about the Bible (e.g., the Bible has all the answers), R829 (20-29, female) at age 22 decided to rededicate her life to Christ "by reading through [the] entire Bible." She hoped the experience would open up new spiritual vistas and deepen her walk with Christ. Instead, the exercise resulted in the first fault line in the foundation of her faith. The Old Testament violence—"too horrible to justify"—repulsed her. At the end of her study, she concluded that if "parts of the Bible [in this case, the stories about God commanding genocide] were true," she couldn't believe in God, and if untrue it would be impossible for her "to believe any of [the Bible]." R457 (30-39, male) recounts a similar experience, which occurred while he was majoring in counseling at Denver Seminary: "[T]he theology classes were the beginning of the end. As I became more aware of the higher criticism and what was simply untrue (but still taught) everything started to crumble." The faith of R395 (30-39, female) "came crashing down over a period of a year," during which time she tried and failed to "convince [herself] that the Bible was inspired." For her, as for many other fundamentalists, it was an either/or answer: "The only two choices (as I saw them) were fundamentalism [or] total disbelief in the Bible as a holy text." A conservative-fundamentalist approach to the Bible leaves no room for compromise and the first doubt often leads to many more. According to R1269 (50-59, male):

> The accumulation of contradictions I began finding as I read the Bible fully through three times before graduating senior high started the process. I'd been taught to take the scriptures literally, and so I did—and began finding that this outlook could *not* [emphasis his] withstand some very basic thinking. That led to doubting the literalist viewpoint. . . . In following years, my studies finally cracked through the dam for any literal reliance on the Bible . . . [M]y own studies of just the basic contradictions pretty well got that process going; higher criticism only reinforced my understanding of scripture's human origins. . . . Those dynamics together [with studying world religions] dampened my reliance on Christianity first and eventually theism in general.

There is a lesson here, for those who have ears to hear. The politicians call it "setting expectations." The political class is well known for publicly underestimating their success in upcoming primary elections, for example, to better position themselves should they actually win the vote. If a politician self-confidently proclaims that he or she is going to be a party's nominee it often does not set up a self-fulfilling prophecy effect but instead establishes expectations too high—and the only place to go from there is down.

The point for the church: CEF ministers do their congregation a disservice when they set up unreachable expectations about the Bible, as witnessed in the account of R1368, and many others, who feel bereft when they finally get around to actually reading the text on which their religion allegedly is based. CEF ministers, therefore, need to set expectations on par with the realities of the Bible. It is highly likely that CEF Christians will encounter these ideas about biblical errors and contradictions at some point in their lives, not often from Ingersoll himself but from those who feel as Ingersoll did. CEF ministers do their congregations a grave disservice by *overstating* the Bible's trustworthiness and by exaggerating the role of the Bible in the life of faith of the church; and by doing so, CEF ministers inadvertently contribute to the falling away (thus my subtitle).

While the Bible is not, in my view, what Ingersoll in the 19th century and Dawkins and others of the New Atheist movement these days make it out to be, it also is not what Moody Bible Institute and Bob Jones University and Focus on the Family and Liberty University claim it is. Fundamentalist claims about the Bible, so easily subverted by even a cursory understanding of biblical criticism and textual analysis, even by an honest reading of the English texts, give birth to a creed that is easily shaken, precisely because it is built not on the rock of evidential fact but on the sands of speculative half-truths. This is clear from the FCNA survey.

Some FCNA respondents described years of study and prayer and counseling and more study and more prayer and more counseling as they struggled with the deconversion process. Most indicated that the emotional upset of learning that the evidence does not support biblical inerrancy was a contributing factor. The Bible, for them, did not live up to its advertising; expectations had been set far too high. Hard as it was, they could not escape the emerging reality: Theism, once so natural, was now against *their* new nature.[20]

Even with that truth accepted, abandoning their faith traditions was difficult: "I almost had some kind of breakdown. [After losing faith], my mind couldn't decipher what was real and what wasn't." (R1332, 30-39, female). A few had an easier time of it and took it all with matter-of-fact certainty: "My deconversion happened exclusively from reading the Bible. Over the course of three months I read every word of the Bible and went from Christian to atheist" (R1347, 30-39, male). But nearly all agreed that the doctrine of inerrancy of scripture, once discovered to be unsupportable by objective evidence, kindled the flame that became a conflagration that burned away their former devotion to a denomination and the Christian religion: "If you are to believe that the Bible is the inerrant word of God or even that it was written under divine inspiration, then it only takes one mistake for that belief to crumble" (R1281, 18-29, male).

Loss of faith in the Bible often leads former CEF Christians to turn to a new source of truth—science.

---

[20] And that's another study waiting to be done—how theism is natural for most but unnatural for some.

Figure 4: T-shirt, www.zazzle.com. Bumper stickers available, too. (Gray scaled for print.) This image is copyright of its owner(s) (if applicable) and is used solely for historical and scholarly illustrative purposes.

Chapter IV

Killing God: Science

Accepting evolution as true was the first nail in the Christianity coffin. —R1494, 50-59, female

Twenty-year-old Leo Chrysostom Behe is one of nine children. He shares a middle name with church father and fifth-century archbishop of Constantinople, John Chrysostom. He was raised and homeschooled in a devoutly Catholic home, with nightly rosary, punctual confession, and regular mass. His mother is a contributor to the *National Catholic Register* and a senior writer at *Faith & Family Magazine*.[21] His father, Lehigh University biochemistry professor Michael Behe, is an architect of the Intelligent Design (ID) movement and author of several books and essays supporting ID, including his most influential works, *Darwin's Black Box: The Biochemical Challenge to Evolution* (1996) and *The Edge of Evolution: The Search for the Limits of Darwinism* (1997). Leo was reared to be a true believer in the faith of the fathers and the faith of his parents, and he followed suit—until he was 17, when young Behe rejected the claims of

---

[21] According to Celeste Behe's Facebook page, www.facebook.com/profile.php?id=1369922400, accessed 28 August 2011.

the Christian faith and all theistic philosophies as untenable. Recently, he "came out" publicly as an atheist in an interview published in *The Humanist*.

Behe's loss of faith commenced in 2008, he says, when engaged in an exercise designed to polish his skill in Christian apologetics—reading (and hoping to refute) Richard Dawkins' *The God Delusion*. To Behe's surprise, Dawkins' strong denunciations of the reliability of scripture undermined Behe's heretofore-untested faith:

> The point that hit me hardest while reading was the fallible origin of Scripture, which I had never considered (to my own surprise). That point in particular was what originally shook my specific faith—Catholicism—and planted seeds of skepticism, which continued to grow as I expanded my knowledge through other literary works on both sides of the issue. (Shaffer n.pag.)[22]

During the struggle with faith and doubt, Behe, in his words, "had no choice" but to "vindicate" his own beliefs through "research, literature, and countless hours of deep thought." It was during these dark nights that his effort to bolster his faith and his belief "in any sort of God" simply "faded away":

> [T]o this day I continue to find more and more convincing evidence against any sort of design or supernatural interference in the universe. As for the arguments from design, such as irreducible complexity

---

[22] Unless otherwise noted, the interview in *The Humanist* is the source for all information about Leo Behe.

> [his father's primary contribution to the field of ID] or the so-called fine-tuning of the six cosmological constants, I have many reasons for dismissing them each in particular, but one overarching reason would be the common refutation of William Paley's classic watchmaker argument—the only reason that complex objects appear to be designed is because we as humans create complex objects, and we then assume that complexity is indisputably indicative of a designer. (Shaffer n.pag.)

The work of his formidably intelligent father notwithstanding, it was Leo Behe's study of the natural world that convinced him that ours is a *godless* creation. And Behe is not the first young believer to be surprised to learn the *scholarly* take on the origins of the Bible and of life on Earth—and to discover that loss of faith in these traditional doctrines of the Christian faith sometimes leads, somewhere down the road, to agnosticism and atheism. The abundant opportunities provided by the Internet, to hear, watch, and read arguments against traditional Christian beliefs, have hurried up the pace of doubt's spread. In pre-Internet days it was possible to live one's entire life without being directly confronted with the convincing arguments of science and biblical criticism. Today, both are accessible at thousands of websites with a few keystrokes. Even with the truth of science readily available to anyone with an internet connection, CEF Christianity continues to wage a battle against science in general and origins studies in particular. There is, after all, a lot riding on both. Conservative Christians at Kentucky's Creation Museum are in fact right: If there is no need for a Creator, everything religious—absolutely everything—is open to reconsideration.

The problem for religious faith is that when science provides an answer for a former mystery, there's one fewer gap for God to hide in. The battle lines, therefore, have been drawn and, for now at least, CEF Christianity is not ceding much to what it often regards as materialistic (by that they mean *godless*) science.

The data from the FCNA Survey reveals that a literal creation event, like the one described in the opening chapters of Genesis, held sway among only 15% of non-CEF Christians prior to their deconversion (see Question 16). Devout CEF Christians, however, accepted the Genesis story of creation as literally true at a rate more than three times that of non-CEFs— 59.8%. And 85.2% of former CEF Christians believed in either the Genesis-literal or Genesis-as-metaphor accounts of creation, meaning that while some conceded that the Genesis account might not be literally accurate, they held to the view that it describes a literal act of divine creation. Former non-CEF Christians were in fact three times as likely as former CEF Christians (37.4% to 13.8%) to select option three when asked what their views were about Genesis during the time they were Christian (see Question 12): "Everything was created by God, but Genesis is a metaphor for God's creative work." This is the view held by evangelical Christian and former head of the Human Genome Project Francis Collins, who has written that it is indeed quite possible and scientifically reasonable to believe in traditional evangelical Christianity *and* in biological evolution at the same time. (See, for example, Collins' 1997 book, *The Language of God: A Scientist Presents Evidence for Belief*.)

Post-deconversion, not unexpectedly, over 95% of all former Christians who responded to this survey concurred with the view of naturalistic science that "life on Earth came to be by natural means"—97.6% of former non-CEF Christians and 96.2% of former CEF Christians held this view.[23] Only about one-fifth of all former Christians who completed this survey reported that accepting that there are reliable non-theistic explanations for the origin of life was "not part of the process" leading to their deconversion. Among non-CEF Christians, 63.3% report that understanding and believing in evolution was a "very important" (36.7%) or "somewhat important" (26.6%) consideration in prodding them along to agnosticism or atheism (see Question 19). Among former CEF Christians, that number is even higher, with 67.5% claiming that being convinced of the reliability of evolution as the only mechanism required to produce life on Earth played a "very important" (42.2%) or "somewhat important" (25.3%) role in their deconversion. The more literally these former Christians previously had read the Genesis creation narratives, the more likely the science behind evolution theory negatively impacted their faith quotient.

While the first challenge to faith for many former Christians is the discovery that the Bible is not inerrant, the topic of origins is usually close behind: "I lost my faith in the Bible *before* [emphasis mine] I accepted the possibility that evolution was true" (R1524, 40-49, male). For some, however, the first prompting of doubt comes not as a result of loss of

---

[23] I assume that the one former CEF Christian who chose the answer that God created everything as Genesis says and the one that chose "God created everything but Genesis is a metaphor," either did so inadvertently or simply aren't quite as convinced of atheism as they thought they were.

faith in the Bible but in the acceptance of the confirming reliability of science: "[I] took a geology class and finally realized that the Earth and the Universe [are] older than what is described in the Bible. I thought if [the Bible and my ministers] were wrong about something as important as that, what else could they be wrong about?" (R1480, 18-29, male). R1390 (40-49, male) added that he always enjoyed watching televised nature programs and when one program narrator offhandedly remarked about human ancestors who "came down from the trees" he began a thorough study of origins, in order to defend his faith in divine creation. After "about a year" of research, however, his belief in the Genesis account of origins was shattered: "I eventually realized that evolution was true. I also believed if this one core belief of Christianity (creation) wasn't true then the rest of it must be bunk."

Some begin the questioning-and-doubting process early in life. R754 (18-29, female) was just six years old when she told her mother that she believed that human life "started out on planet earth as ooze or fungus," *not* as a unique creation of God. The budding scientist was not rewarded for deep thinking but was, quite literally, sent to her room. She also remembers that as a youngster and early adolescent she read everything she could get her hands on about the theory of evolution, even though she "couldn't discuss this at home" for fear of parental disapproval.

For many, of all ages, simply put by one respondent, "evolution changed everything" because "[i]t's so beautiful to see the mechanism which creates such wonderful things without the need for magic [meaning, the supernatural] of any kind" (R1545, 18-29, female). The beauty of evolution notwithstanding, often getting from point A (divine creation) to point B (materialistic evolution) is a circuitous route: "I went through all the stages: biblically literal creation as a young child, day-age theory as a young adolescent, and increasingly more liberal intelligent-design ideas as I got older until God fell out of the picture entirely" (R1161, 18-29, female). Forty-something male R822 likewise didn't skip a step along the path from top-down creation to bottom-up evolution: "I went from creationist to watchmakerist to metaphorist to agnostic to atheist."

While a cornerstone of the sciences, especially biology, evolution of species is not the whole cloth. Science is about freedom of inquiry, the right to ask questions, the possibility of objectively testing hypotheses, the judgment of peer review, revision of theory in the light of new evidence, an unbiased analysis of the material universe without supernatural interference or superstitious inhibitions. It is how we moderns understand our world, how we know what the weather might do over the next twenty-four hours and how we seek a cure for cancer and AIDS and heart disease and Alzheimer's.

But CEF Christianity remains in opposition to the modernizing and enlightening effects of science. It abides by the King James translation of Paul's admonition to his "son in the faith": "O Timothy, keep that which is committed to thy trust, avoiding profane and vain babblings, and *oppositions of science falsely so called* [italics mine]: Which some professing have erred concerning the faith" (1 Tim. 6.20-21a.) The Greek word translated "science" in the KJV is γνῶσις *(gnōsis)*, translated "knowledge" in just about every other translation. Paul's warning here in fact may have been against an early

Gnostic group. It was not a warning against twenty-first century science. However, the KJV was the dominant Bible in the English-speaking world for four centuries after its initial publication in 1611 and, therefore, what most readers likely took away from this passage was the idea that "science falsely so called" (also translated thusly in the Geneva Bible of 1560) was a detriment to the faith, a viewpoint that has not waned, a view that remains strong among some CEF Christians. This was the case with R304 (40-49, male), who reports that he and his co-religionists were "taught that science was the devil's way of tricking us." R504 (18-29, male) was also part of a religious group that marginalized (again, to quote the KJV) "science falsely so called": "My views of science were always repressed. [E]very time I learned something I was told that it was wrong. I loved science growing up and eventually learned to keep my scientific beliefs a secret because at that time it was hard for me to defend them."

The suspicion of science among some CEF Christians can be disastrous. It almost cost R575 (30-39, female) her life. Even suffering from asthma, she was told by her faith leaders to stop taking her allergy and asthma medications "because those ailments were a trick," designed "to test" her faithfulness. Her ailments were "in [her] head" and God "would heal" them if she "were a better believer." Doggedly following her faith leaders' admonitions resulted in a three-day asthma attack that almost killed her before she was rushed to the hospital by one of her school teachers. At the ER, she was found to have a disturbingly low oxygen count; she remained in the hospital for a few days before, fortunately, a full recovery. After this horrifying and near-deadly experience, "it wasn't hard," she writes, "to switch over to believing in science." She had discovered that in her recent life-and-death situation "praying doesn't do a single thing, but medication sure does!" She had learned what R1479 (40-49, male) proposes: "We can't accept the scientific method when it prevents or treats diseases, makes our cars run better or feeds millions of people and turn around and reject it when its conclusions diverge from our most cherished religious beliefs."

Prior to deconversion, former CEF Christian respondents to the FCNA Survey (see Question 20) were quite likely (60.9%) to adopt a position that science "had its place," that it "should not overstep that place," and that when science and religion contradicted one another, "Bible truth trumped scientific truth." Among non-CEF Christians, that number dropped steeply to only 16.1%. Non-CEF Christians, prior to deconversion, were much more likely to adopt a position similar to that of Stephen Jay Gould's Non-overlapping Magesteria (NOMA), doing so 57.2% to 32.2%. CEF Christians, therefore, encounter many more challenges to their Bible-based worldview. They find it more difficult to live peacefully with the demands of a scientific age, sometimes to the extent of avoiding science. Many respondents report that when they were CEF Christians, they were "not that interested in science" (R1359, 60-69, male, who now "can't get enough" of science); and that they had "refused" to understand scientific fields such as "evolution and genetics" (R1333, 30-39, male). R829 (18-29, female), when a Christian, had "a fundamental misunderstanding of science" and, therefore, "deeply mistrusted scientists," rejecting out of hand any "supposed evidence of evolution" as "either misunderstanding or misrepresentation of data on the part of the scientific community."

Now deconverted, 71.9% of former non-CEF Christians report that an increased understanding of science and the reliability of the scientific method were either "very important" or "important" in their deconversion; and slightly more former CEF Christians report likewise: 75.7%. Only 16.7% of former non-CEF and 14.6% of former CEF Christians claim that improved understanding of science was "not part of the process" that led to deconversion. Likely, most of these who claim science was not a factor in their deconversion are those who had a more friendly relationship with science in the first place, those for whom science seemed natural and real, even during their years in the CEF movement, such as R1468 (30-39, female): "I was always a science girl. Evolution was always the answer for me, so it wasn't a tough leap to go from god started it to the big bang. . . But later becoming a full on atheist, science had a tremendous role in my rejection of the god hypothesis." Another former CEF Christian who also was science-friendly during her years as a Christian is R1494 (50-59, female), who wrote: "I always enjoyed playing with bugs when I was a kid and loved all things science, but I had to keep 'two minds' about it—one for church and one for what I was seeing. I had to grow up and get away from the family before I realized I needed only one mind."

R1494 and her compatriots in the ex-Christian movement were formerly among the true believers, the faithful, the set apart, safe in their insular faith against all outward storms. But the storms came anyway, and the wind blew against their faith, and, for some, the battering winds were origins studies or genetics or the hard sciences: "Cosmology had the most influence in my deconversion and it became the foundation for my scientific views. The change was difficult, extremely mentally painful, and I faced persecution and rejection on many sides socially" (R990, 30-39, male). But science has a way of overcoming. "Science," writes R1052 (18-29, male) "was the major factor in my movement away from Christianity. Without science, I would probably still be preaching." Science, starkly put by R538 (40-49, male), "destroyed my Christian faith/theology."

Their deconversion in the past, safely behind them, the experience itself often is told with the same vigor and drama and sense of predestination as those of a Sunday night testimony meeting. Writes one: "Once I started research on origins of the Old and New Testaments, reading scientific articles and books by authors like Stephen Hawking, Brian Greene and others, *it was as if a deep hunger was finally being satisfied* [italics mine]. This wonderful journey took me about ten years" (R1518, 60-69, female). While the source of inspiration has changed for these former Christians, the need for occasional inspiration, a revival of sprit, remains, and science meets the need: "Watching Carl Sagan's *Cosmos* is like a religious experience for me. I watch it beginning to end at least a few times a year" (R1100, 30-39, male). Science allows many of these individuals for the first time to trust their senses, to trust what they always knew to be true: I had to "learn to trust my own mind and believe that science is a noble profession rather than a tool of the devil. . . . I ended up seeing science as a collection of great thinkers who had their own resistance to superstition in pursuit of reason" (R1273, 60-69, male).

As with hard literalism in regard to the Bible, CEF Christianity's insistence that science is intentionally at war against its interests is counterproductive. While indeed science can and will and must eliminate superstition, it does not have to eliminate all varieties of faith. The Bible is not and was never intended to be a science textbook, no matter what the Texas State Board of Education might say. CEF leadership must acknowledge this reality and ease up, in fact totally abandon warfare against science, if it is to survive. To stubbornly resist modernity and the blessings of science is not wise and is not spiritual. And it is not beneficial to the aim of religion, which is supposed to be helping all human beings live a happy and free life, at peace with themselves and their neighbors. CEF leaders need to listen to the testimony (if I may call it that) of R303 (40-49, male): "The more I learned of science, the less the Bible could be accepted as anything more than interesting stories. As the religion I was in was very much in the literal tradition, the tension was very high, in the end, science . . . could not be denied." By teaching a less literal version of the Bible's "interesting stories" and by setting the congregation free to pursue science where science takes them, the "tension" between modernity and pre-modern tradition eases and all members of the household of faith are better able to "walk in thy truth" (Ps. 86.11, KJV), even if that truth is discovered by science.

I am not, personally, a believer or a religious man in any sense of institutional commitment or practice. But I have enormous respect for religion, and the subject has always fascinated me, beyond almost all others (with a few exceptions, like evolution, paleontology, and baseball).

Stephen Jay Gould, "Nonoverlapping Magisteria," 1997

Figure 5: "All-American Church of the Religious Right," David Horsey, *Seattle Post-Intelligencer*, 2004. This image is copyright of its owner(s) (if applicable) and is used solely for historical and scholarly illustrative purposes.

Chapter V

Killing God: Conservative Politics

I struggled with conservative Christian viewpoints and eventually came to realize that I did not share the same political sensibilities as the rest of the congregation.
—R1265, 60-69, female

The story is well known. The American people are a religious clan. They always have been. The Mayflower Compact, written in the fall of 1620 while that ship of Christian pilgrims was anchored in Provincetown Harbor, was a God-filled document. The voyage from the Old World to the new one, the Compact proclaimed, was "undertaken for the glory of God, and advancement of the Christian Faith" (as well as "the Honor of our King and Country").[24] Two hundred years later, the fabled Frenchman Alexis de Tocqueville (1805-1859), after spending two years in America, wrote with charm and insight about the religiosity of the American people of the early 1830s. (More on that later.) Abraham Lincoln, near the end of the four-year tribulation period that was the American Civil War (1861-65) composed the closest thing to Gospel any American president has ever

---

[24] Modern spelling.

written—the Second Inaugural Address, brimming full of religious imagery, biblical quotations, and theological thoughts on why the fratricidal war came upon the land. A century later (1955), a great-grandson of slaves, twenty-six-year-old Martin Luther King (1929-1968), newly appointed minister at the Dexter Avenue Baptist Church in Montgomery, Alabama, took up the Hebrew prophets' spirit-inspired refrains about peace and social justice and led a Sermon on the Mount-based movement, centralized in the Southern *Christian* Leadership Conference, against the power of southern pharaohs and "cows of Bashan,"[25] like George Wallace, Bull Connor, and scores of be-patient white ministers like those in April 1963 who prompted the writing of King's splendid gospel, "Letter from Birmingham Jail."

But something changed in the 1970s and 1980s. The shift was fundamental. While in former days, the liberal-progressive religious *were* involved in every social movement to emerge from American soil, and political leaders were free to speak their minds on issues religious (more or less, excluding of course someone publicly taking a razor to the Bible, which Thomas Jefferson did *privately*), there existed an American doctrinal consensus, a civil contract, that excluded the religiously-motivated from seeking to overtly impose their religion on the American government.[26] Jefferson's interpretation that the First Amendment ("Congress shall make no law respecting an establishment of religion or prohibiting the free exercise thereof") created a "wall of separation"

---

[25] Amos 4.1

[26] One might be able to argue otherwise in regard to the temperance and prohibition movements.

between church and state was universally accepted.[27] Martin Luther King, after all, did not seek to inspire a political party to take over the American government and do things his way. He wished to liberate human hearts from the bondage of racism and the drum-beat of war in Vietnam by means of the spiritual tactics of civil disobedience and passive resistance, inspired, of course, by Jesus, Henry David Thoreau, and Mahatma Gandhi. Even the fundamentalists of the first half of the twentieth century were far more concerned about influencing their denominations' policy-making plenaries than in telling Congress what to do to save the nation's soul. Before the 1970s, fundamentalist Christians held firmly to their heavenly citizenship and, other than voting, didn't involve themselves much in the affairs of *this* world.

By the end of the 1970s, however, evangelical Christians emerged as a strong social and political force in American politics. Jimmy Carter (president, 1977-1981) was a moderate Southern Democrat when he eagerly outed himself as both someone who lusted in his heart and as a "born again" Baptist

---

[27] Jefferson's masterful articulation of the doctrine of separation of church and state, found in an 1802 letter to the Danbury (Ct.) Baptist Association, is worth quoting in full: "Believing with you that religion is a matter which lies solely between Man & his God, that he owes account to none other for his faith or his worship, that the legitimate powers of government reach actions only, & not opinions, I contemplate with sovereign reverence that act of the whole American people which declared that their legislature should 'make no law respecting an establishment of religion, or prohibiting the free exercise thereof,' thus building *a wall of separation between Church & State* [italics mine]. Adhering to this expression of the supreme will of the nation in behalf of the rights of conscience, I shall see with sincere satisfaction the progress of those sentiments which tend to restore to man all his natural rights, convinced he has no natural right in opposition to his social duties." ("Jefferson's Letter to the Danbury Baptists")

Christian. After the corruption of the Nixon administration and the ho-hum interregnum of the Ford years, America longed for a president who promised not to lie to them—and backed it up with an impeccable reputation and a Sunday school teacher pedigree.

But Carter honored the wall that had been placed between government and religion. Many CEF Christians did not. The 1970s witnessed the rise of the Moral Majority and its founder, Jerry Falwell, who single-handedly defeated the Equal Rights Amendment (ERA) and declared war on the "liberal justices" who in 1973 handed down *Roe v. Wade*. Another CEF Christian voice of that era was the self-proclaimed spokeswoman for righteousness, Anita Bryant, who commanded a crusade against gays and lesbians, in order to save America from the fiery fate of Sodom and Gomorrah.

Out of the tumultuous decades of the 1960s and 1970s was born in the 1980s, for the first time in America, a politically engaged CEF Christian movement that overtly, even from the pulpit, urged its members to vote for the right person, as a Christian duty and moral obligation. By the end of the Reagan years in 1989, the Republican Party only slightly resembled the party of Teddy Roosevelt and Dwight Eisenhower. It had been overwhelmed by conservative, evangelical, and fundamentalist Christians. By the end of the 1980s, one could not be a candidate for the American presidency without proclaiming love for God and the Bible.[28]

Of course all citizens have a right to participate in this democracy and all have a right to evangelize their beliefs and

---

[28] President Ronald Reagan and the U.S. Congress proclaimed 1983 the "Year of the Bible."

values and goals, but the 1990s was a decade in which some within CEF Christian denominations believed that their views were the only correct ones, not because the evidence proved such but because, they told us, either God or the Bible (or both) advocated for those views, too. The 1990s emerged as an era of proof-text politics. The days Alexis de Tocqueville observed in the early 1830s were long gone:

> [T]he American clergy stand aloof from secular affairs. This is the most obvious but not the only example of their self-restraint. In America religion is a distinct sphere, in which the priest is sovereign, but out of which he takes care never to go. Within its limits he is master of the mind; beyond them he leaves men to themselves and surrenders them to the independence and instability that belong to their nature and their age. . . . All the American clergy know and respect the intellectual supremacy exercised by the majority; they never sustain any but necessary conflicts with it. They take no share in the altercations of parties, but they readily adopt the general opinions of their country and their age, and they allow themselves to be borne away without opposition in the current of feeling and opinion by which everything around them is carried along. They endeavor to amend their contemporaries, but they do not quit fellowship with them. Public opinion is therefore never hostile to them; it rather supports and protects them, and their belief owes its authority at the same time to the strength which is its own and to that which it borrows from the opinions of the majority. (*Democracy in America* 28-29)

Recently, *Foreign Affairs* magazine (March/April 2012) published an essay by Notre Dame political science professor David E. Campbell and Harvard professor of public policy

Robert D. Putnam on the religio-political landscape of the United States during the last four decades, the period during which the Republican Party acquired a "fervently religious base" (35), when "moral conservatives banded together to fight the Equal Rights Amendment, gay rights, and abortion" (37), and to establish "a godlier government" (39). Called "God and Caesar in America," the article's subtitle suggests the authors' thesis: "Why Mixing Religion and Politics is Bad for Both." They argue that today's partisan divide "pit[s] religiously devout conservatives against secular progressives" (34, 35) and has precluded the possibility of another era of good feelings[29] such as the one booming (in regard to offspring *and* economics) in the 1950s: "[I]n President Eisenhower's America, religion had no partisan overtones. Ike was as popular among those who never darkened the door of a church (or synagogue, and so on) as among churchgoers" (36).

Campbell and Putnam suggest that the hyper-partisan and hyper-religious nature of American politics has soured younger Americans on religion in general and CEF Christianity in particular: "Just as the 1960s spurred a revival of traditional religion, the last few decades have led directly to an unprecedented turning away from organized religion, especially among younger Americans" (41). They further assert that this pulling away from religion is a "correlation" that is "causal, not coincidental" (34). It is "primarily" (their word) due to the emergence of the "religious right." In the last two decades, they note, sociologists and historians of religion

---

[29] My summation phrase, not theirs. The first Era of Good Feelings, a period of bipartisan cooperation and national unity, was during the James Monroe administration of 1817-1825.

have observed among the young a steady decreasing interest in adopting a religious identity:

> The best evidence indicates that this dramatic generational shift is primarily in reaction to the religious right. Politically moderate and progressive Americans have a general allergy to the mingling of religion and party politics. And millennials[30] are even more sensitive to it, partly because many of them are liberal (especially on the touchstone issue of gay rights) and partly because they have only known a world in which religion and the right are intertwined. To them, "religion" means "Republican," "intolerant," and "homophobic." Since those traits do not represent their views, they do not see themselves—or wish to be seen by their peers—as religious. (42)

Most of the respondents to the survey of former CEF Christians—64.8% of them—were under 40 years old. It is precisely the under-40 demographic that came of age in the 1970s and 1980s, the period in American history that witnessed both the politicization of religion and the religionization of politics. It is the under-40 crowd that Campbell and Putnam reference in the *Foreign Affairs* essay. The FCNA survey data support Campbell and Putnam's proposition: younger people are less likely to associate themselves with a religion that is overly political, and certainly less likely to align with CEF churches that are politically conservative, especially in regard to social issues.

---

[30] Not defined in this paper, but often designated as the "eighties babies," or Generation Y, following Generation X.

The survey data reveals that membership in any Christian denomination has a tendency to foster more conservative political views (see Questions 24 and 25). The before- and after-deconversion data across the board shows a decrease in conservative views and an increase in liberal views, whether the former Christians were previously affiliated with liberal or conservative Catholic or liberal or conservative Protestant churches. Among the former non-CEF respondents to the FCNA Survey (1170 individuals), only 9.9% described themselves as "very liberal" prior to deconversion; now 35.3% do. Among these same respondents, the percent claiming "conservative" or "very conservative" political leanings dropped from 22.3% prior to deconversion to 3.8% after. The data for former CEF Christians (391 of the FCNA respondents) is even starker. Prior to deconversion, only 1.8% were "very liberal"; now, 35.8% are. If we combine the "very liberal" and "liberal" choices among former CEF Christians, only 7.9% claim such prior to deconversion, while a whopping two-thirds (67%) do so now. In the clearest evidence of the conservative political milieu of CEF Christianity, 72.4% of those who responded to this survey were "conservative" or "very conservative" *prior* to deconversion, while only 4.8% claim such post-conversion. (That sentence deserves to be read again.)

In looking at the data for the 2008 presidential election (see Question 28), among those who were eligible to vote (U.S. citizens) and did so, Senator Obama triumphed in a landslide. Among non-former CEF respondents, 63.6% voted for Obama/Biden; 3.9% voted for McCain/Palin; and 32.5% were either ineligible to vote (non-U.S. citizens), did not vote, or voted for a third-party candidate (often the Libertarian). Among former CEF Christians, in 2008, 60.9% voted for Obama/Biden; 7.4% for McCain/Palin; and 31.7% were ineligible to vote, did not vote, or cast their vote for a third-party candidate. If these 1,561 respondents are an accurate indication, deconverted Christians are quite *unlikely* to vote for a Republican (i.e., conservative) presidential candidate. Among all non-CEF respondents who were eligible to vote (U.S. citizen, at least 18 years old) and voted for one of the two major party candidates, Obama/Biden garnered 94.2% of the vote, while McCain/Palin were not even in double-digits, at only 5.8%. Former CEF Christians were slightly more likely to vote McCain/Palin (10.9%) than were former non-CEF Christians and slightly less likely to have voted Obama/Biden (89.1%).

The data for the 2012 election was collected prior to the election in November. It reveals a similar intention among respondents. Former non-CEF Christians planned to vote as follows: 59.8% for President Obama; 5.3% for the Republican nominee; and 34.9% are ineligible to vote, will not vote, or will vote for a non-two party candidate. Former CEF Christians remained, early in 2012, overwhelmingly for Obama: 60.6% for Obama; 5.9% for the Republican nominee; and 33.5% ineligible, not voting, or voting for a third-party candidate. While in 2008, CEF respondents voting for one of the two major candidates were more likely to vote Republican than their non-CEF counterparts, this election season, the numbers have evened out. Non-CEF respondents voting for one of the two parties' candidates intended to do so at 91.9% for Obama and 8.1% for the Republican nominee; while among former

CEF Christians, Obama would collect 91.2% of the vote and the Republican nominee 8.8%. The comparable responses between former non-CEF and CEF Christians might indicate that former CEF Christians in the interim between 2008 and 2012 have become slightly more liberal in regard to American politics.

While it is incontrovertible that nearly all former Christians who are now agnostic and atheist have abandoned conservative politics (the data are overwhelming), determining if this correlation is causal is another matter. Campbell and Putnam believe it is "causal, not coincidental"—that is, conservative politics in the church *causes* some to reject not only the politics but the religion with which they are associated (34). In the FCNA Survey (see Question 27), respondents were asked if their personal adoption of more moderate or liberal political positions than those of their former denominations' leaders and members played a role in their deconversion and, if so, how large a role. While about half of all respondents said that their personal political liberalization was not part of the deconversion process, about half claim that it was, even if, for some, "not that important." Among all former non-CEF Christians, 28.7% believe that their moderate-liberal political views in opposition to the conservative views of their denomination and religious cohorts played a "very important" or "somewhat important" role in their deconversion process. Among former CEF Christians, that number is higher—37.6% responded that the gulf between their more moderate or liberal views and the conservative views of their denomination played a "very important" or "somewhat important" role in their disenchantment and eventual deconversion. And former CEF

Christians were *less* likely than the other groups to report that politics played no role in their journey from belief to unbelief, with 42.5% claiming it was not part of the process (compared to 51.5%). It would seem, therefore, that indeed while politics as a larger category is not a primary factor in deconversion for most, it is a factor of some note for at least half of the respondents to this survey.

Among the more heated controversies currently erupting in the Christian world is that of the proper place of homosexuals in religious *and* civil society. Conservative Christians remain overwhelmingly opposed to full and equal inclusion of gay and lesbian persons in the culture[31] at large and, especially, in their denomination's leadership. It seems prudent, therefore, to spend a few moments analyzing the role of conservative politics in the deconversion process by spending time considering this particular issue: homosexuality and the church.

While 45% of the former non-CEF Christians who responded to the FCNA Survey report that even while they were Christian they held a "very liberal" or "liberal" view of homosexuality, only 13% of former CEF Christians report such (See Questions 30 and 31). Among former CEF Christians, 24% had a "moderate/centrist" view of homosexuality and were not sure what they thought about the issue prior to their deconversion; and 62.9% formerly had a "conservative" response and were "uncomfortable" with gay persons or were

---

[31] In the two years since this thesis was written, rapid changes have occurred. Gay Americans are far more welcome in the culture in 2014 than they were in 2012. Conservative Christians, however, remain in a holding pattern, attempting for at least a little longer to preserve their ancient beliefs.

"very conservative" in their views about sexuality and knew and believed all the anti-gay "clobber verses" of the Bible.

Post-deconversion, the respondents to this survey have overwhelmingly liberalized their response to sexual minorities. While 45% of former non-CEF Christians were "very liberal" or "liberal" in their views about homosexuality when they were Christian, after deconversion these two categories ("very liberal" and "liberal") claim 97.5% of respondents. Among former CEF Christians, the portion claiming a "very liberal" or "liberal" view of homosexuality when Christian, a mere 14%, has grown to include 95.9% of former CEF Christians who are now agnostic or atheist. Only 1% of former CEF Christians remain "conservative and uncomfortable" (none is "very conservative") about homosexuality, compared to 62.9% who were "conservative and uncomfortable" about homosexuality before deconversion. The evidence on this subject is abundantly clear: The Christian religious are generally more conservative politically than agnostics and atheists and the Christian religious are much less likely to openly accept homosexual persons as civil or spiritual equals. Conservative Christianity fosters conservative attitudes about homosexuality.

A review of the data in the FCNA Survey *by declared sexual orientation of the respondents* reveals a more varied and interesting picture (please see Questions 30 and 31, responses by sexual orientation). Among the "exclusively" and "primarily" heterosexual (of all former Christian groups), prior to deconversion only 33.2% had "very liberal" or "liberal" views about homosexuality, while (surprisingly) the "exclusively" and "primarily" homosexual were only slightly more accepting—with 35.2% claiming "very liberal" or "liberal" views about homosexuality prior to deconversion. Interestingly, sexual minorities themselves prior to deconversion were more likely to be less accepting of other sexual minorities. Bisexuals, for example, were more likely to fall into the "very conservative" and "knew all the 'clobber verses' by heart and believed them" categories, at 11.3%, followed by those who are exclusively homosexual, at 10.9%. Only 6.2% of exclusively heterosexual and 5.8% of the primarily heterosexual persons placed themselves in the "very conservative" descriptor category. While Christian, therefore, heterosexuals were *less* likely than bisexuals or homosexuals to have "very conservative" views about homosexuality; and, surprisingly, it is the exclusively homosexual who were more likely than any other group to have had "conservative" or "very conservative" views, with 40.6% of the 64 claiming such. After the deconversion process, over 95% of all respondents are "very liberal" or "liberal" in their acceptance of homosexuality—96.2% of the exclusively heterosexual; 98.4% of the primarily heterosexual; 99% of the bisexual; 97.2% of the primarily homosexual; and 100% of the exclusively homosexual and asexual.

Of all non-CEF respondents, 53.5% claim that their more liberal views about homosexuality were not part of the deconversion process (see Question 33); and 41.2% of former CEF Christians also claim that this was not a motivating factor. But 58.9% of former CEF Christians claim that their liberalizing views about homosexuality did indeed contribute, at least somewhat, to their deconversion: 18.2% say this was "very important" in the deconversion process; 18.4% say "somewhat important"; and 22.3% report it was an issue, albeit "not that important." If one looks at the data by sexual orientation of the respondents (see Question 33, responses by sexual orientation), it becomes evident that having views about homosexuality that were more tolerant or liberal than their denominations' doctrines and co-religionists played a much larger role, not surprisingly, in the deconversion process for sexual minority respondents. While only 8% of those who are exclusively heterosexual claim that the dichotomy of views played a "very important" role, 37.1% of those who are primarily homosexual make this claim, and a super-majority of 67.2% of those who are exclusively homosexual feel that the issue of homosexuality was an important factor in their decision to deconvert. Sexual minorities, therefore, are more likely to either abandon their conservative Christian churches for more liberal Christian churches or, as in the case of the respondents to this survey, for agnosticism and atheism, than are those of the sexual majority, in part on the basis of their emerging understanding of their own minority standing.

This survey did not ask of heterosexuals who among them, when Christian, had close friends or family who were gay or lesbian. If it had, likely those who did were more likely than those who did not to have distanced themselves from their denomination on account of disagreements regarding the status of homosexuals in the church. As one respondent (R1563[32], 50-59, male, exclusively heterosexual[33]) put it: "Knowing

---

[32] While the FCNA Survey was completed by 1,561 individuals, another four began the survey but did not finish it. Their responses are not included in data, but are included in the response number; thus, it is possible as in this case to have R1563, even though actually only 1,561 completed the survey.

[33] Only during this section discussing homosexuality will the self-

homosexuals personally changed my view." Exclusively heterosexual thirty-something male, R1462, wrote that the more he got to know a particular homosexual friend, "the harder it was" for him to "think of him as 'hellbound.'" Traditional Christianity teaches that sexual minorities, at least their sexual acts, are abominations. The constant pounding on the pulpit to denounce homosexuals reinforces and sanctifies anti-homosexual prejudice: "As a Christian," says R1530 (30-39, male, exclusively heterosexual), "it would probably be fair to say I hated homosexuals to some degree. I was taught disregard for gays, and I used my religion to justify how I felt."

When congregants begin to understand the world differently and in ways outside the comfort zone of their religious leaders and fellow churchgoers, it often provokes both personal anxiety (about being led astray from the true faith, for example) and gnawing doubt about the rightness of the faith (if the faith can be wrong about one thing, it can be wrong about another). As one respondent's views of homosexuality liberalized, compared to those of his denomination, he was torn: "I struggled with the way my faith was making me act like a jerk" (R1500, 18-29, male, exclusively heterosexual). One bisexual (R1492, 18-29, female) wrote thusly:

> I always knew I was attracted to women, and it was agony for an outsider homeschooled smart-but-awkward kid to put all my life's purpose and work into something that told me over and over that I was somehow horribly flawed. I tried to see counselors, to talk to people, to pray away the gay, as they say, but it

---

identified sexual orientation of respondents be divulged.

didn't work, and the process horrified and disgusted me. . . . Honestly, losing religion was such a weight off my young shoulders. Suddenly I wasn't a freak and a sinner, doomed to a vice I couldn't seem to shake, but instead I was a normal young person who fell in a normal spectrum of human behavior, accepted by sociologists and psychiatrists and other scientists worldwide.

Respondent 1489 (18-29, female, primarily heterosexual) perhaps speaks for many who experience similar cognitive dissonance when hearing their ministers instruct on a truth that they no longer believe:

I sat in church one Sunday and the pastor called homosexuals an abomination in the eyes of God. It ripped my heart to shreds, as I saw the face of each and every one of my homosexual friends flash through my mind. I thought to myself, how dare you! How dare you sit in judgment of your fellow human beings! . . . I couldn't justify aligning myself with his view of homosexuals, and this played a massive part in my deconversion.

While some who responded to this survey indicated that neither liberalized views on politics or homosexuality played a significant role in their deconversion (for a few, these played no role at all), most indicated that the opposite was true: "My views on homosexuality were a defining moment in my deconversion," said one (R1375, 30-39, male, exclusively heterosexual). "[The issue of homosexuality] is another example where I found the Christian religion and the Bible to be immoral," wrote another (R1368, 30-39, male, exclusively heterosexual). An 18-29-year-old heterosexual male (R953) was adamant: "I have always been accepting of homosexuals and most Christians here (West Michigan) aren't, despite the Christian teaching of 'love thy neighbor.' This obscene self-contradiction was another reason I rejected Christianity." R894 (30-39, bisexual woman) wrote that "the single biggest issue in my rejecting Christianity was knowing full well that I, in my natural state, was bisexual. If I was created deliberately by god, why would he create someone he would hate? Once you step outside and look at it, the Christian mythos falls apart." Exclusively homosexual thirty-something male R1100 reports that it was the gay question that dealt the fatal blow to his faith: "[C]oming to accept that homosexuality is not evil was the primary impetus for my losing religion." Primarily heterosexual thirty-something male R931 reports that the harsh condemnation of homosexuality by his church was the most important cause of his starting the deconversion process: "If I had to pick a single cause for my deconversion, this would be it." R659, an 18-29 primarily heterosexual male, puts it bluntly: "Politics were a big thing at church. Rejecting one meant rejecting the other." And thirty-something exclusively heterosexual male, R404, summarized in four words the cause of his religious and political deconversions: "I hated hating people."

Making the issue of status of gays an even more pressing one that CEF Christianity must accommodate is this statistic (see Question 8): Respondents choosing "exclusively heterosexual" as their sexual orientation were the least likely of all groups to have been "very interested in religion" prior to age 18, with only 29.4% claiming such, while bisexual respondents were the most likely to have been "very interested in religion" (47.4%) prior to 18, and following closely behind were the exclusively homosexual, with 45.3% describing themselves as "very interested in religion" prior to age 18. Among the exclusively and primarily heterosexual, 20.3% claim to have had *no interest* in religion prior to age 18, while only 13.5% of those exclusively and primarily homosexual make this claim. The sexual minorities who responded to this survey were more interested in religion at an earlier age than were those of the sexual majority.[34] Respondents to this survey who are exclusively and primarily homosexual were also more likely to report a previous affiliation with CEF Christianity (31.3% reporting such) than were the exclusively and primarily heterosexual (23.3%). This question needs to be studied more extensively, of course, but it seems that bisexuals and homosexuals are more likely to exhibit interest in religion at an

---

[34] Anecdotally, this was the case in the rural Pentecostal church I was affiliated with in my mid- to late-teens. The heterosexual boys were hardly interested in church, while the four young men most involved, faithful, and loyal were homosexual or bisexual. One became a pastor in the (gay) UFMCC and another became a Pentecostal preacher who married a woman and had two children before "coming out" and divorcing.

[35] Paragraphs 2357-2359: Homosexuality refers to relations between men or between women who experience an exclusive or predominant sexual attraction toward persons of the same sex. It has taken a great variety of forms through the centuries and in different cultures. Its psychological genesis remains largely unexplained. Basing itself on Sacred Scripture, which presents homosexual acts as acts of grave depravity, tradition has always declared that "homosexual acts are intrinsically disordered." They are contrary to the natural law. They close the sexual act to the gift of life. They do not proceed from a genuine affective and sexual complementarity. Under no circumstances can they be approved. . . .Homosexual persons are called to chastity. By the virtues of self-mastery that teach them inner freedom, at times by the support of disinterested friendship, by prayer and sacramental grace, they can and should gradually and resolutely approach Christian perfection.

earlier age than heterosexuals *and* they are more likely to associate with CEF denominations than are their heterosexual counterparts. This possibility alone should motivate CEF Christians to perform a soulful re-evaluation of doctrines about homosexuality.

It has been widely reported, and hotly disputed, that a disproportionate number of Roman Catholic religious (priests, monks, and nuns) are homosexual, with estimates varying widely, but generally estimated at between 10% and 40%, far surpassing the proportion in the general population. The Catechism of the Roman Catholic church[35] may define homosexuality as "intrinsically disordered," and homosexual acts as examples of "grave depravity," but evidence would seem to indicate that there are many homosexuals who play key roles in the hierarchy of the RCC. I suspect that this is true in other Christian traditions as well, all the more reason to step outside of one's doctrines for a moment and allow sexual minorities to speak. The recent Third Way movement might allow both sides to engage a cease-fire: a Third Way church neither accepts nor condemns sexual minorities; instead, it suspends judgment, allows all equal rights to participate, without making definitive doctrinal statements on the issue.

It is clear that for many of the deconverted, political conservatism and social intolerance toward the Other helped cultivate the doubts and questions and cognitive dissonance that would eventually play a significant role in their decision to abandon CEF churches and, ultimately, the Christian religion. According to one respondent (R1233, 30-39, female, primarily heterosexual): "[T]he church's intolerance was probably one of the first things to put me off." Many others indicated similar experiences and reported that their church's social and political conservatism was among the reasons they deconverted. Bringing the issue of conservative politics and gay prejudice and the role each plays in the deconversion process to a conclusion is done perfectly by thirty-something, primarily heterosexual female R1233:

> My church's stance on homosexuality was one of the first things that really came to bother me. I met a gay classmate in high school. I found that he had the same issues and same experiences with his partner that I had with my boyfriend. He clearly loved in the same way that I did. I saw nothing wrong with his behavior and feelings, and I couldn't understand what was so bad. After meeting him I immediately rejected my church's stance on homosexuality. I actually became angered by it. My father was, and continues to be, seriously homophobic. It divides us still. I believe churches should be pro-love and pro-marriage. I cannot understand the hatred toward LGBT . . . Voting pro-gay is very important to me as an adult.

Congress shall make no law respecting an establishment of religion or preventing the free exercise thereof, or abridging freedom of speech, or of the press, or the right of the people peaceably to assemble and petition their government for a redress of grievances.

First Amendment to U.S. Constitution

Figure 6: "Damaging Winds," James MacLeod, commentary on the May 2011 tornado that killed ca. 160 in Joplin, Missouri, www.facebook.com/MacLeodCartoons. This image is copyright of its owner(s) (if applicable) and is used solely for historical and scholarly illustrative purposes. Used with permission.

Chapter VI

Killing God: Earthquakes, Tsunamis and Hellfire

> *Jesus, were you just around the corner?*
> *Did you think to try and warn her?*
> *Or were you working on something new?*
> *If there's an order in all of this disorder*
> *Is it like a tape recorder?*
> *Can we rewind it just once more?*
> —"Wake Up Dead Man," U2, *Pop*, 1997

It has been argued that the religious impulse is born of the human need to explain or understand or appease suffering, particularly the pain we experience at the deaths of those we love and the hollowness and anxiety many feel in running head on into their own mortality. Once the gods were created—to adopt for a moment the theory that holds to a strictly naturalistic origin of religion, *à la* Daniel C. Dennett's *Breaking the Spell: Religion as a Natural Phenomenon*—they (the gods) were forced to play a role in the human drama of life and love and loss unfolding among all beings. Perhaps Zeus was displeased with Mr. Smith or Thor was angry at Mrs. Smith, which explains why that terrible thing happened to them when they fell off a cliff and died. Among the Hebrew Bible's primary reasons for being is answering the question of why bad things happen—to bad people *and* to good people. According to all those prophets—Isaiah, Ezekiel, Jeremiah, et al.—there was a reason Israel suffered at the hands of the Egyptians and Assyrians and Babylonians and Greeks and Romans—and that reason was disobedience to the covenant. The Christian religion, which emerged out of the Hebrew tradition, founded by two Jews, Jesus and Paul, evolved a belief that "God is love" and "love is from God" and "God so loved the world" and "the greatest of these is love."[36] Reconciling a God who is the essence of love with enormous human suffering, therefore, became an important endeavor among church fathers and theologians, from the earliest epistles of the mid-first century through the twenty-first century. Much of the first 2,000 years of Christian history was devoted to writing a satisfactory theory of theodicy, meaning an attempt to understand and explain why there is suffering in the world if God is all good and all love.

The scholar Bart Ehrman (former CEF Christian, now agnostic, profiled in an earlier chapter) spent the first half of his lifetime, he writes, attempting to tease out a consistent biblical narrative on the perplexing issue of theodicy. In his 2008 book, *God's Problem: How the Bible Fails to Answer Our Most Important Question—Why We Suffer*, he lays out the *several* biblical answers to that question, finds them *all* hopelessly contradictory and unsatisfactory, and declares the Bible's theories on theodicy largely a failure. There is no reconciling a loving God with the suffering so many encounter

---

[36] I John 4.7,8; John 3.16; 1 Cor. 13.13.

in this life, says Ehrman. It is the presence of suffering and the inability of Christianity to satisfactorily respond to it theologically and psychologically that are among the reasons Ehrman rejected his previous faith and opted to live the remainder of his life as an agnostic.

CEF Christians seek answers for all questions, including the dilemma of suffering, primarily from their "only rule of faith," the Bible. The FCNA Survey (see Questions 35-37), not surprisingly, reveals that former non-CEF Christians were much more likely than former CEF Christians, *when they were Christian*, to accept the perspective that pain and suffering just are, and that there is "no adequate explanation" for either unhappy condition, with 44.2% of non-CEF Christians agreeing with that statement and only 12.8% of former CEF Christians. Nearly half of former CEF Christians, 46.8%, when they were Christian, believed that all pain and suffering were direct or indirect results of the Fall (of Adam and Eve) and continued human error/sin, and that all would be "healed by God in the Kingdom." And 40.4% believed those teachings *and* that some pain and suffering was "punishment" or "chastisement" from God. (A nearly identical 40.5% of non-CEF Christians also believed in the suffering-as-punishment argument.) Once free of biblical constraints, after the deconversion process, these same individuals (now agnostic and atheist) are nearly unanimous in their view that there simply is no "spiritual explanation" for the suffering humans and animals endure—with 99.2% of former non-CEF Christians and 99.5% of former CEF Christians (see Question 36) agreeing with that statement.

While about one-fourth of the former Christians who completed this survey (see Question 38) report that unanswerable questions about pain and suffering and the goodness of God (theodicy) were not involved in their deconversion process (26.7% of non-CEF and 22.3% of CEF), three-fourths report that this thorny issue did indeed play a role. Among non-CEF Christians, 58.9% report that the inadequacy of various theodicy theologies was a "very important" or "somewhat important" consideration in their rejection of Christian theology; among former CEF Christians, 59.7% report that this ancient mystery—why there is suffering if God is love—was among the challenges that eventually snuffed out their faith.

For many of the deconverted who completed the FCNA Survey, this question was only one among many—reliability of the Bible, politicization of their church, treatment of outcasts such as homosexuals, and rejection of the blessings of the scientific method. For these ones, the existence of enormous suffering was simply another wedge between themselves and the idea of a god: "It [rejecting theological explanations for suffering] was a natural extension of my rejection of biblical literalism," reports R958 (18-29, male). For R541 (40-49-year-old male), "[t]he problem of evil was a part of my deconversion, but *only after* [emphasis mine] science had killed most of the fundamentalism."

For others, theodicy was the most pressing issue of all. For fifty-something female R71 it was "the most important factor in my deconversion, and also the most difficult because I spent a couple years trying very hard to reconcile pain and suffering with Christian notions of God. In the end, I could not reconcile this." R490 (18-29, male) also found in suffering a hurdle he could not overcome: "This . . . is probably the single largest factor in pushing me from being . . . Christian."

Many struggled, long and hard, with the deepest and darkest question of all—how a loving God can allow human (and animal) suffering: "This was one of the biggest problems for me as a Christian. I read over 15 books just on this one subject and never found a satisfactory explanation. The suffering of innocent children is unacceptable to me. For a loving God to allow/decree it is unthinkable" (R977, 50-59, male).

Sometimes, world events presented these former Christians with questions they had not previously asked themselves and with theologies, from fellow Christians or church leaders, they could not in good conscience adopt. One young mother was told that her ill newborn was sick "due to a generational sin" (R16, 30-39). A forty-year-old mother of an eight-month old watched the Christmas 2004 Asian tsunami in horror. From the warm comfort of her living room, she saw a news story about an Indonesian mother who "watched all eleven of her children swept away." A few days later, she overheard a Christian friend ask: "I just wonder what those people did to incur God's wrath like that." It was at that precise moment, she reports, that she "absolutely knew that there was no god" (R652, 40-49). The Christmas tsunami was also the catalyst for the deconversion of R798 (30-39, male): "My mother shocked me . . . when she commented that the tsunami of 2004 was the result of sin." From that moment, he recognized that he was "completely at odds with my mother and pastors and friends on spiritual topics"; thereafter, he "inched toward that slippery slope to loss of faith." For one respondent, the moment of clarity and, with it, profession of non-faith, emerged after watching a movie about the young Anne Frank, who died in the Holocaust when her family's secret annex was discovered by the Nazi overlords of occupied Amsterdam. At the movie's end, one haunting question remained: "How can there possibly be a God?" (R135, 50-59, male). A "preacher's glibness about those sufferings" prompted an immediate deconversion for R659 (18-29-year-old male).

The open-ended question on the FCNA Survey revealed loving and sensitive souls simply seeking answers to the question of suffering, and finding none that satisfied them. "In a nutshell, I want nothing to do with a god that would allow such suffering. This played a huge part in my deconversion," wrote R304 (40-49, male). Referencing the theodicy masterpiece that is the biblical writing called Job, a sixty-something female, R982, commented: "This was major in my deconversion. The problem of Job bothered me. If I was distressed by the sufferings of others—how could a loving god not only tolerate it, but bring it about via divine will or plan?" For another young man, the break came when during his college years he read Bart Ehrman's books on the New Testament: "[H]is views on pain and suffering played a large role in my eventual atheist stance" (R121, 30-39).

Many did not describe a specific personal story of pain or that of a loved one or a specific world event, such as an earthquake or tsunami, demolished their belief in a god. Instead, deconversion followed a long-standing erosion of faith in a loving creator after the accretion of decades of doubt about the existence of justice—or even Karma—in this life. For some, the doubt and struggle against suffering and pain was held at bay as long as the pain was witnessed from a distance. When it hit closer to home, however, some awoke to find no suitable answer. The cancer death of one woman's 28-year-old husband "was definitely a catalyst" in the deconversion of now fifty-something R71. A forty-something male, R450, recalls that the murder of his son-in-law followed by the cancer death of his 32-year-old brother-in-law (his "best friend") made him realize that his "fasting and . . . faith were not good enough" to convince God to intervene. Cancer claimed the friend of R1485 (50-59, male), and then it claimed his faith: "Prayers for a friend who had cancer were not answered (many people prayed). Eventually I came to think that Christianity cannot escape the Problem of Evil." A young female (R829, 18-29) suffered terribly as her worldview fell apart and she had no answer for the suffering of life:

> The problem of human suffering gave me the most emotional anguish. I had long been troubled by the pain in my parents' lives (despite their well-lived faith). After I started doubting the Bible, I became much more deeply disturbed by pain and suffering. I had to let go of Heaven, which was one of the most deeply painful aspects of the process. This left me feeling like life was a meaningless collection of painful, pointless years. It took several months for me to begin to discover meaning without God/an afterlife, and I continue to struggle with coping with how painful life really is.

Hellfire

Another type of suffering and pain, one much worse than all the possible kinds of suffering one could experience on this earth, is the doctrine of eternal torment in hellfire. For some former Christians it was this doctrine that first stirred them to a reexamination of faith and a renewed search for truth—that culminated in agnosticism/atheism. Most CEF Christians believe in a literal Hell, a "lake of fire" (to use the language of Revelation[37]), where all the lost—meaning, according to most CEF Christians, all who fail in this life to accept Jesus as Lord and Savior—are confined forever and ever in "outer darkness" where there is "wailing and gnashing of teeth" (Matt. 8.12, KJV). They take this creed with a chilling literalness. Throughout the Christian era, of course, many Christians have dissented from a literal reading of the Bible's hell passages, claiming that these are metaphors for destruction and separation from God or simply descriptors of the grave or warnings about the danger of a godless life. But many denominations have yet to let go of hell and some preachers still use fear of hell as a primary tool of evangelism.

We have discussed two of the assaults on William Lobdell's faith—wickedness in holy paces (the pedophile

---

[37] Revelation 20:10-15 (KJV): "And the devil that deceived them was cast into the lake of fire and brimstone, where the beast and the false prophet are, and shall be tormented day and night for ever and ever. And I saw a great white throne, and him that sat on it, from whose face the earth and the heaven fled away; and there was found no place for them. And I saw the dead, small and great, stand before God; and the books were opened: and another book was opened, which is the book of life: and the dead were judged out of those things which were written in the books, according to their works. And the sea gave up the dead which were in it; and death and hell delivered up the dead which were in them: and they were judged every man according to their works. And death and hell were cast into the lake of fire. This is the second death. *And whosoever was not found written in the book of life was cast into the lake of fire* [italics mine]."

priest scandal) and exposure to higher criticism of scripture. The breaking point, according to his spiritual memoir, *Losing My Religion*, were questions about suffering and the incomprehensible nature of the doctrine of a literal eternal hellfire. This once faithful evangelical Christian began to ask himself some very hard questions:

> Why are some prayers answered directly while others appear to be ignored? When a little girl gets raped and killed, where is God? Why might a busload of Christian high school athletes crash on the highway? Why does God play a hide-and-seek game with us, making it difficult to figure out how He wants us to act? (127)

At the same time, evangelical sermons on the torments of eternal hellfire for non-believers left Lobdell reeling: "Anger welled up inside me when evangelicals talked about how sad it was that people who didn't believe in Christ would be sent to hell" (169).

Unsatisfying theodicy theologies and a literal hell were also "major factor[s]" in the deconversion of R1313 (40-49, female): "God's apparent inability or unwillingness to stop suffering and the idea that He would damn non-believers (or believers of other faiths) who could not possibly be expected to know 'The Word' disturbed me greatly." "How can a loving God allow his children to burn for eternity?" asked R404 (30-39, male). Seventy-something female R850 experienced a similar tug-of-war with faith when she found herself unwilling to "believe in an all-powerful Loving Being that would create us and willingly allow us to suffer unfathomable pain and then condemn us to a fiery inferno for minor infractions of his commandments." Still, for many, it took "many, many years" for agnosticism to win the intellectual and spiritual battle over theism, primarily due to "fears instilled in me from birth." An anger similar to that of R850 was also experienced by R1422 (18-29, female):

> In Bible study, I asked my pastor about Jeffrey Dahmer and Mahatma Gandhi. Dahmer killed and ate little boys. Gandhi was a peaceful man who saved millions. One of them became a Christian right before death and one of them did not. Who did our church believe was in heaven? My pastor, without hesitation, said Jeffrey Dahmer, since he accepted Jesus Christ as his savior just before death. So, Dahmer could go to heaven . . . [while] Gandhi went to hell because he believed in the wrong god?

If it wasn't higher criticism or scientific literacy or conservative politics that lodged in the minds of former Christians, and often it was all three at different times and to different degrees, the problem of evil and suffering and eternal punishment stacked up against an allegedly long-suffering and loving "Our Father" did. As reported by the former Christians who completed the FCNA survey, there are too many examples of clergy and laity poorly equipped to squarely face these eternal questions—sometimes faltering, sometimes ignoring the problem, and sometimes haughtily speaking harsh and hurtful words about the pain of others. For many fundamentalist Christians, therefore, a literal understanding of God's sovereignty results not in peace but in disappointment, when evidence accumulates against the hypothesis/doctrine. The letdown means that one more support beam in the edifice of faith comes tumbling down. CEF leadership, largely, seems unwilling to do what is necessary to be a helpful voice in times of suffering, pain, and death. Until they re-examine pat answers to human suffering and clichéd theories about pain, until they admit that sometimes God is (or at least certainly seems) far removed from human suffering and that they, too, struggle with understanding why cancer wards are full of children, their explanatory theologies are nothing more than sounding brass and tinkling symbols, they offer no consolation to an individual going through a dark night of the soul, and they provide one more good reason to be agnostic about things religious.

Figure 7: T-shirt of the OutCampaign.org, http://www.zazzle.com/atheist_out_campaign_tshirt-235341851287525839, accessed January 15, 2012. (Gray scaled for print.) This image is copyright of its owner(s) (if applicable) and is used solely for historical and scholarly illustrative purposes.

Chapter VII

Coming Out Atheist

Our choir is large, but much of it remains in the closet. Our repertoire may include the best tunes, but too many of us are mouthing the words sotto voce with head bowed and eyes lowered. It follows that a major part of our consciousness-raising effort should be aimed, not at converting the religious but at encouraging the non-religious to admit it — to themselves, to their families, and to the world. This is the purpose of the OUT campaign.

—Richard Dawkins, in 2007, announcing the OUT Campaign

Richard Dawkins is right. Agnostics and atheists must learn from the example of gays and lesbians. If they wish to advance their right to full inclusion in the lives of their nations, agnostics and atheists must "come out" and openly confront a largely theistic world. As long as doubts are left unsaid and those who don't believe in all the, in their view, hocus-pocus, keep silent and don't make waves, agnostics and atheists will remain the least popular group among us.

According to a study published in the *American Sociological Review* in 2006, homosexuals, Muslims, and atheists generally round out the list of Americans who are least trusted, least likely to be elected president, and least likely to be met with joy at the news of impending marriage to one's child (Edgell, Gerteis, and Hartmann). Other more recent surveys reveal that atheists in America experience more social ostracism than Muslims *and* homosexuals. The tide is turning, however, in large part due to increased willingness among agnostics/atheists to reveal themselves, especially among the under-30 cohort.

Various social media outlets, such as Facebook, make the "coming out" process for all sorts of hidden minority groups (gays, lesbians, transgender, atheists, etc.) much easier than it ever was. All one need do is post one status update to his or her Facebook page and in a couple of hours everyone—from parents to peers and colleagues and siblings—knows one's perspective. And that's why the "Out Campaign" of the Richard Dawkins Foundation for Reason and Science[38] has been in full swing since 2007, urging all agnostics and atheists to be out about their non-beliefs and to recognize that they are not alone: "Atheists are far more numerous than most people realize. COME OUT of the closet! You'll feel liberated, and your example will encourage others to COME OUT too."

The OutCampaign language is verbatim recapitulation of that of gay campaigns, such as National Coming Out Day (founded in 1988): Coming out can "demolish the negative stereotypes of atheists. Let the world know that we are not about to go away and that we are not going to allow those that would condemn us to push us into the shadows." And just like

---

[38] www.OutCampaign.org

the LGBT community, atheists embolden themselves and empower their group by seeking common ground with the larger population. From the OUT Campaign: "We come in all shapes, sizes, colours and personalities. We are labourers and professionals. We are mothers, fathers, sons, daughters, sisters, brothers and grandparents. We are human (we are primates) and we are good friends and good citizens. We are good people who have no need to cling to the supernatural."

The OUT Campaign encourages agnostics and atheists to place a bumper sticker on their cars, to open up about their views, even to proudly wear a scarlet "A"—for atheist (see Figure 16). Following in the footsteps of every American social movement since World War II, seculars and "nones" and agnostics and atheists recently marched on Washington—the Reason Rally of in March 2012, billed as "the largest gathering of the secular movement in world history" (see Figure 17). Among the purposes of "coming out" and "reason rallies" and Internet campaigns for agnosticism / atheism is to defy stereotypes, such as "the angry atheist." While there *is* a website called AngryAtheist.com, most atheists do not fit the bill and to counter false impressions, one atheist even runs a successful blog called "The Friendly Atheist" (see Figure 18).

Losing faith in God can be traumatic and depressing and it usually disrupts social networks organized around shared spirituality. No longer believing in the supernatural even causes fear and anxiety for some:

> My journey from extreme religious to extreme non-theist and back to an atheist middle ground[39] has taught

---

[39] For some, of course, atheism is not "middle ground." For this respondent, however, it is.

me that giving up religion is tough. The experience was so emotionally stressful that I thought my world would literally end (and, had a few key friends not been there for me during my few months of transition from god-believer to non-god-believer, I would likely not be typing this right now). Through experience, I know all too well how fragile religion is. One question from a trusted friend is all it really took for atheism to root within my religious frame. Once I began to doubt religion, the entire system fell apart along with my moral compass and emotional grounding. I would not personally wish the experience upon anyone. (R1438, 18-29, male)

A sense of foreboding, of fear, for some even terror, was described by many as common emotions experienced during the deconversion process. R1395 (30-39, female) reports that it took her "at least a decade" of a "difficult transition" before she could "become comfortable with the thought that everything I believed as a child was a lie," and for her to truly know with certainty that she was not "turning [her] back on God."

Among former non-CEF Christians (see Question 40), about one-fourth (25.9%) reported that the transition from theist[40] to agnostic/atheist was "not difficult at all"; among former CEF Christians, however, only half that fraction reported thusly—just 12.0%. Among former non-CEF Christians, 14.4% found the deconversion "very difficult" and 28.3% found it "somewhat difficult." Most former CEF Christians, those who had held more tenaciously to their religious views, found the process of deconversion "very

---

[40] One who believes in a god.

difficult" (40.9%) or "somewhat difficult" (30.7%)—meaning that for three-fourths of them, the journey was a difficult one.

Respondent 505 (18-29, male) is a former CEF Christian who in the FCNA Survey selected "very difficult" to describe his deconversion. He expounded on his experience thusly: "Losing my faith was miserable and horrific and lonely and painful. I lost everything, including a Christian woman who meant the world to me." Another male, in his forties, likewise endured a tumultuous deconversion experience and has yet to "come out" to his father and relations: "The change was heart-wrenching at times, seeing friends become extremely worried about my immortal soul and no longer being in the xtian[41] (un)reality bubble. Took me about 40 years to partially come out of the atheist closet, and am still not out to my dad or most of my relatives" (R822). The FCNA Survey reveals that 77.7% of former non-CEF Christians are "out" to "everyone" or to "most friends and family . . . including . . . parents"; slightly fewer former CEF Christians are as "out" about being agnostic or atheist—72.7%. Nearly one-fourth (22.3%) of former non-CEF Christians are more guarded about their agnosticism/atheism and have only told "some friends" and "some family" but not parents; among former CEF Christians, that number is a bit higher, at 27.4%.

Some new agnostics and atheists are fortunate to have supportive families and friends, whose love is unconditional. R865 (30-39, female) tells her coming-out story like this: At her sister's 27th birthday party, she came out to her sister, divulging her atheism. The sister's reply: "I know." She asked

---

[41] It seems that some former CEF Christians prefer to write "xtian" instead of "Christian."

her sister if their mother and father already knew that she is atheist. Her sister's calm reply: "We've known for a very long time." The lifelong lack of interest in religion had been obvious to her discerning parents and sister and they were simply waiting for their daughter/sister to tell them on her own timetable: "So they knew it before I even knew to call myself that. There just was a severe disinterest in religion. It provided nothing to think about, at all. I found myself attracted to science and math. My family doesn't care that I'm this way and I don't care that they still practice." Another respondent (R1492, 18-29, female) wasn't so lucky:

> I'm not sure which was harder, though: coming out to my parents about being gay or telling them I was an atheist. But you simply couldn't be in the church without accepting the sinfulness of homosexuality or the obvious moral imperative of pro-life thought. It was some of these thoughts that started me questioning the veracity of the holy book in the first place; should I believe God is right and I'm wicked for having these thoughts about women, or are they outdated/wrong, undermining the whole of the Bible?

We all need occasional fellowship with a group of likeminded people, those we can count on for an understanding ear. This is especially true for "others," the ones who don't quite fit in. Coming out publicly and knowing other publicly out agnostics/atheists is helpful and offers an outlet for voicing one's frustrations and disappointments. Among former Christians, socializing with former Christians, it creates an opportunity for social relations with others who perfectly understand the process one endured to arrive at a place of peace and acceptance.

This is, in my view, another area in which CEF churches can do better—blessing their enemies (so-called) instead of cursing them; welcoming them and their non-belief into their lives; and making an effort to get to know the "others" around them—those who have other gods, those who are LGBT, those who don't believe in things supernatural. It might not be easy, but Christian "love of neighbor" demands it. So does the future of the faith. If religionists wish to remain in the mainstream, and not on the Westboro fringe, accommodations must be made. After all, didn't Jesus hang out with the "others" of his day—publicans and prostitutes, Samaritans and sinners?

Figure 8: "Blind! Idiot! Rat Fink!," cartoon by Don Addis (1935-2009). This image is copyright of its owner(s) (if applicable) and is used solely for historical and scholarly illustrative purposes.

Chapter VIII

Dear John Letters to the Church

"Be more like Christ and less like Jerry Falwell."
—R118, 30-39, male

The final question of this survey gave former Christians an opportunity to speak to their former denominations or to the Christian church in general. The prompt read: "If you were to advise your former denomination (or the Christian church in general) about how to be better, how to be more relevant, how to keep up with the times, what would you recommend? (Abandoning belief in a god/God is not likely; what other recommendations would you offer?)" Of the 391 former CEF Christians who completed the survey, 366 responded to this question.

A few would have none of it, void of any desire to offer recommendations to their former faith family: "I have nothing to say to them beyond fuck off" (R27, 30-39, male). Another commented that "conservative Christians" are "bigot[s]" and "closed minded asshole[s]," not worthy of his advice (R286, 18-29, male). One bluntly asserted: "I don't want them to be relevant and I don't want them to . . . keep up with [the] times and therefore be more attractive to some people. I want them gone. I want a world free of religion. Sorry, no advice from me" (R1513, 18-29, female). A thirty-something female wrote that her former church is "so backward and so proud that nothing I could say would have any bearing . . . I really don't see how churches can be any more relevant than Santa Claus or the Tooth Fairy . . . I think Harry Potter or Lord of the Rings has more to teach us than the Bible" (R221). And one young male (18-29 years old) summed up his view with three words: "Go to hell" (R650), while a thirty-something female used four words: "Throw out the Bible" (R1252). Perhaps speaking for several, one respondent unleashed a furious attack, born likely of the pain of his own deconversion—an attack which, on second thought, he tried to contain with an admission that the intensity of his anger is "very wrong":

> Go away and die. Stop infecting the world with your poisonous lies. Just standing in the same room with you makes me sick. You probably became a minister just to dodge the draft. How many lives did you ruin just to make your own a little more comfortable? I hope you feel every ounce of pain you've cause others tenfold. Seriously, fuck you. This is why I just keep my distance. I admit that I am very wrong in this way of thinking. I just haven't finished dealing with that pain yet. (R427, 30-39, male)

Most, however, offered heartfelt—and sometimes urgent—advice to the Christian church, along five lines of thought: abandoning fundamentalist interpretations of the Bible; accepting evolution as fact; ending the enmity against science; avoiding conservative social politics; and nurturing tolerance and acceptance of atheists, homosexuals, and members of other religions, thereby eliminating what is perceived by these respondents and by many others to be a reflexive response to non-conformity that is "ultra judgmental" (R1552, 18-29, intersex/transgender).

Former CEF Christians believe that the Bible is "allegory" and "myth" and, therefore, must be taken "figuratively" (R1563, fifty-something male). They know that Christian denominations will not abandon the doctrine that the Bible is at the very least a divinely inspired document. They do, however, suggest that CEF Christians "have an open mind" when they read the Bible (R1535, 18-29, male), that they "abandon literalism" (R1492, 18-29, female), and at least "reconsider" their view that "the Bible is the true and unaltered and perfect word of god" (R1490, 18-29, female). "Admit that the Bible isn't perfect," says one (R1182, 30-39, male). Only by "reinterpret[ing] the Bible from scratch" (R911, 40-49, male) and "[r]ead[ing] the Bible as you would any other book, from start to finish" without accepting on faith "what you were told it says" (R562, 40-49, male) can the church find its way out of the easily challenged conundrum of biblical literalism, says another. Perhaps R25, a forty-something male, summed up perfectly the view of former CEF Christians, now agnostics and atheists: "Don't look at the Bible as infallible. Look at the Bible as a book of philosophy [and] be willing to adapt the philosophy of the Bible to new information."

The former CEF Christians who responded to this survey are equally strident in their recommendation that their former faith fellowships "drop the hostility to science" (R1552, 18-29, intersex/transgender) and accept that "the Bible is wrong regarding things like evolution" (R1489, 18-29, female). They urge all Christians to accept as fact that science is the only arbiter of truth and reality that can be shared by all human beings. Most former CEF Christians have spent significant time, formally and informally—while Christian, during the deconversion process, and post-deconversion—becoming scientifically literate. "Do not deny science," demands one, for "it only makes you look ignorant and [then] when people discover the truth they are more likely to leave the church than if you had told them about it in the first place" (R1187, 30-39, male). Instead of denying the power of science, it should be allowed to "lead the way," insists another (R990, 30-39, male). Christians who want to "make the god-did-it claim" (R504, 18-29, male) are free to do so, but denying any claim of science only weakens the religious structure and, ultimately, as history teaches, religion must cede ground. It is better, therefore, to surrender to science what is science's: "There is room to say the universe works by scientific principles and still have a God who set up those principles" (R498, 18-29, male).

The data reveal unequivocally that former CEF Christians are in agreement about one thing—the politically conservative domination of CEF Christianity is an albatross that must be overcome, if the church is to remain relevant in an America in which tolerance of homosexuals, social diversity, and religious pluralism is gaining ground—notwithstanding these final bursts of protest from conservative Christians. These former CEF Christians insist that current CEF Christians must "be less judgmental" (R1494, 50-59, female) about The Other and they must stop "pushing their beliefs on others" (R1505, 50-59, female). They must break the bonds between CEF Christianity and the political right: "Remember to follow the Golden Rule, and keep your faith out of politics. Don't try to legislate or bully your beliefs onto others" (R1162, 40-49, male). One former CEF Christian, a thirty-something male, quoted his former savior, Jesus, in insisting that CEF Christians need to "focus on their [spiritual] beliefs and not on politics" because "Jesus' kingdom is not of this earth" (R719). Christians must "drop all pretention of superiority over those of different racial, sexual, or political orientations" (R326, 30-39, male). Several of these respondents insisted that all religious attempts to disenfranchise the LGBT community in America must be abandoned: "Accept that homosexuality is natural and not a sin" (R1100, 30-39, exclusively homosexual male). But the constant refrain for these former CEF Christians is that Christians in America need to "get out of politics" (R193, 50-59, male) and stop "assum[ing] that God is a Republican" (R6, 30-39, male). Another, more bluntly: "Stop watching 'The 700 Club' and Fox News" (R871, 40-49, male).

Former Christians they are, and more than anything else these agnostics and atheists want CEF Christians to be what they claim to be—Christian. They want them to live up to the highest ideals of their faith: "Do not convert people by your words, but by your actions," wrote one (R1062, 40-49, female), in what might have been an intentional paraphrase of the words (falsely) attributed to St. Francis: "Preach the gospel at all times, and when necessary use words."[42] Another encouraged the members of his former denomination to "love all people for

---

[42] While ubiquitously quoted as a teaching of St. Francis, there is no evidence that he actually used these words. See, for example: Galli, Mark. "Speak the Gospel: Use Deeds When Necessary." *ChristianityToday.com*. Christianity Today, 21 May 2009. Web. 30 April 2012.

what they are" (R1000, 50-59, male), while another summed up his view thusly: "Try not making judgments, after all that's what Jesus said: 'Judge not, lest ye be judged'" (R629, 30-39, female). One young man (18-29) called for tolerance, albeit a bit crudely: "Stop being dicks to everyone with a different opinion" (R515). Another respondent made the same call, even more crudely: "Stop being so fucking hateful" (R702, 18-29, female). Channeling the spirit of the teachings of St. Paul himself, two former CEF Christians wrote lovingly and tenderly, and movingly:

> Heed the Sermon on the Mount more than Deuteronomy; loving thy neighbor is a far better witness than pointing out the mote in your brother's eye. . . . Remember humility and compassion and brotherly love. None of us is so great we cannot fall. And almost all who have fallen can be redeemed, if not by religion, then by common human grace. Forgive the past. Enjoy the present. Hope for the future. Judge sparingly, forgive often, and love always. (R239, 40-49, male; R480, 30-39, male)

Former Christians want what we all want: the right to be left alone; the right to live life fully; the right to be free to think, to learn, and to grow, even if that growth means they cannot follow their former religion without doing harm to their consciences. They don't mind religion, per se, or the religious; they simply wish to see their former brothers and sisters in the faith free to believe in science, including biological evolution, free to hold political opinions that don't satisfy Ralph Reed or Franklin Graham or the leaders of American Republican Christianity, and free to love all their neighbors—yes, even the

Hindu and gay and atheist ones. If the responses to this final survey question are an indicator of what former CEF Christians want, it seems that they stand shoulder to shoulder with Thomas Jefferson: "I have sworn upon the altar of God eternal hostility against every form of tyranny over the mind of man."

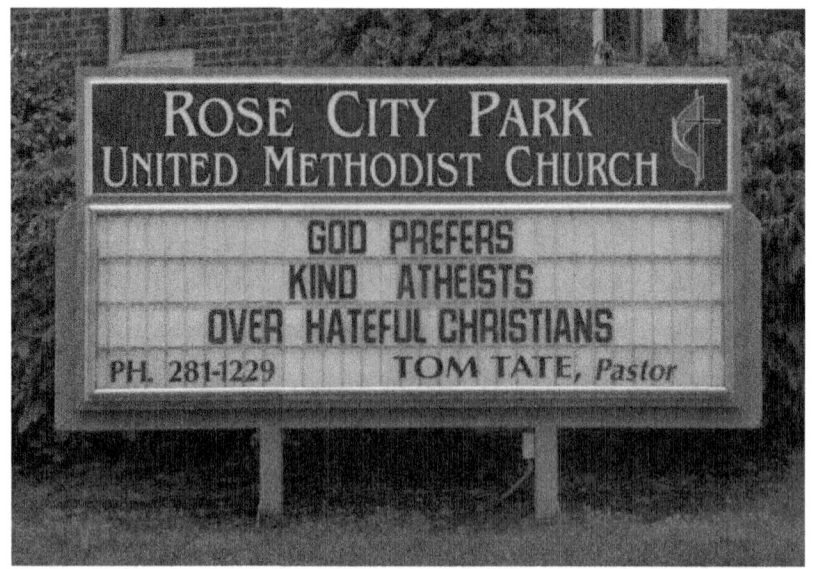

Figure 9: This image appeared all over the Internet, posted hundreds of times in various social media outlets, including Facebook, and Twitter. To the best of my knowledge it is a photo of the church marquee of the Rose City Park United Methodist Church in Rose City, Oregon and originally may have appeared in *The Oregonian* in 2012. (Gray scaled for print.) This image is copyright of its owner(s) (if applicable) and is used solely for historical and scholarly illustrative purposes.

Chapter IX

Conclusion

A new commandment I give unto you, That ye love one another; as I have loved you, that ye also love one another. By this all men shall know that ye are my disciples, if ye have love one to another.

—Jesus (John 13.34-35, KJV)

Human beings come in all sizes, shapes, and colors and they adopt all manner of views and opinions and responses about everything under the sun. What is art to one, is trash to another. One person's gourmet dinner, is slop for another's swine. Opera enraptures some and puts others to sleep. Some are born with faith, others acquire it, some never find it, and some end up letting it go. No one can ever say that the process that put us here—purposeless evolution or a purposeful Creator or both or neither—doesn't like diversity.

In this study, we have examined the spiritual histories of 1,561 former Christians who are now agnostics and atheists. They once believed, with all their hearts.[43] In time,

---

[43] And, by the way, they want their former friends and family who remain religious to stop demeaning their experiences by claiming that they never really believed anyway or they could not have deconverted.

circumstances and a thoughtful, sincere study of the claims of their faith and the claims of science and philosophy and the evidence as they see it made it impossible for them to maintain a theistic orientation, without disobeying their minds and cauterizing their consciences. They had to go. Like the theologian in training, Peter Fromm, in Martin Gardner's novel, *The Flight of Peter Fromm,* they outgrew their faith and had to flee. It no longer made sense. They now stand firmly on the side of "no-god," and they do so not to antagonize those who believe, but because they cannot do otherwise. They are not, for the most part, out to get anyone (sometimes I wonder about Richard Dawkins, frankly). They simply adhere to the truth as they perceive it and, perhaps, they still believe that their former savior, Jesus, was right: "Ye shall know the truth, and the truth shall make you free." (John 8.32, KJV)

Many former Christians go through a period of mourning over the loss of their old friend faith and for some it is an agonizing struggle: "The change was difficult, I'd rank it up there with losing a friend or sibling" (R713, 40-49, male). Some feel regret about time lost believing something they now find preposterous: "It was very difficult because my entire youth had been founded in the absolute perfection of the Word of God, and I wanted so much to believe" (R1349, 40-49, female). For some, loss of faith is nothing short of devastating: "Letting go of God was one of the most agonizing torments I've ever experienced. My sense of purpose was lost and . . . I felt very alone" (R403, 18-29, male). A few, such as 18-29-year old female R1203, continue to struggle with the loss of faith: "I will readily admit that it's a struggle to maintain positive feelings about being alone in the universe after believing the contrary for so long."

Given time, however, most reconstitute their personality, *sans* the supernatural, and emerge whole and free (there's that word again): "I concluded feeling refreshed and liberated," wrote one (R1351, 50-59, male). Some do become, temporarily at least, as annoying in their "evangelism" for no-faith as they had once been evangelists *for* faith. Admits one: "I know that I was a fundamentalist asshole as I entered college, but did not make it a full two years after that before I was an atheist asshole" (R97, 30-39, male). A few, as we learned in Chapter VII (Coming Out Atheist) remain "in the closet" about their rejection of theistic philosophies. Some just keep it to themselves. And some are "out" to friends and even some family, but not to their beloved parents, their first teachers in the faith, the ones they least wish to disappoint. A few remain skeptical that their no-faith journey, while intellectually honest, is the answer to the world's problems: "I would not, and do not, try to deconvert Christians. I am not at all sure that my 'brave' recognition of the facts of life and death makes for a better life than their belief that they are children of God who will live forever" (R186, 40-49, male).

What one is taught in youth is mighty difficult to outgrow. Learning that the fairytales of childhood, taught so lovingly on Mom's knee, are just that, fanciful tales, is disappointing. Is anyone happy to discover that there really is no Santa Claus? But religious doctrines, believed with one's whole heart, soul, might, and mind mean so much more than the Santa Claus story. Santa shows up but once a year. God is supposed to be (to paraphrase some Bible verses) a friend who sticks closer than a brother, an ever-present help in time of need, always with us even until the end of the age. Religious doctrines are about life and death, peace and joy, where one spends eternity, how one might be able to rejoin deceased loved ones.

When a pre-pubescent girl or boy discovers a toy in mom's closet and later finds that same toy under the Christmas tree, with a "From: Santa" gift tag, it can pierce the heart.[44] Discovering that the Bible is not quite what a loving Sunday school teacher said it was or not quite as reliable as a favorite preacher claimed, also pierces the heart—*and* the soul. Santa Claus is magnified ten thousand times in God.

What if, therefore, CEF churches abandoned biblical inerrancy? What if they stopped teaching that the Bible is the perfect Word of God? Would not doing so serve as an inoculation against the loss of faith that often follows the inevitable discovery that the Bible does not quite live up to that worshipful praise? And couldn't they frame that doctrinal evolution as reclaiming the ancient faith of the first century when after all *there was no Bible*, at least not as we know it today, when to early Christians Jesus was the Word of God, not a book, when Paul was dashing off letters that I'm convinced he had no idea would one day end up in a collection called scripture. (I suspect he would be horrified!)

Those who accept gay persons as equal citizens with equal rights and dignity find it hard to continue attending a church that preaches otherwise. Eventually, they leave that church and find another one or they leave the Christian religion altogether, if that issue coupled with others makes staying Christian a

---

[44] Personal experience speaking here.

violation of conscience. It seems clear that if the Christian church, speaking primarily of the CEF church here, wishes to find a way to continue to speak to the under-40 crowd and certainly to the under-20 crowd it must drop conservative politics and polemics against homosexuality. It must no longer be true that "there's no place to learn hate like a Sunday school classroom" (R427, 30-39, male). So what if CEF Christians stopped teaching that God is a Republican and that God wills the death of homosexuals as, if you read the Bible from a conservative/fundamentalist mindset, God appears to do in Leviticus 20:13[45] and Romans 1[46] and I Corinthians 6:9[47]? Abandoning the anti-gay rhetoric surely would be better for their congregations, for the men and women who sit in their pews and have LGBT children and nieces and nephews and enjoy watching "Modern Family" and "Glee."

Full legal equality for gay citizens in America, including marriage equality, is around the corner. [Note: It happened in 2015.] Why not get ahead of the curve, preach inclusion (instead of exclusion) and acceptance (instead of rejection) and, thereby inoculate CEF believers from the cognitive dissonance that follows when they hear their pastor preach against gays on Sunday night and still enjoy watching sweet

---

[45] "If a man also lie with mankind, as he lieth with a woman, both of them have committed an abomination: they shall surely be put to death; their blood *shall be* upon them." (KJV)

[46] Specifically verse 32: "Who knowing the judgment of God, that they which commit such things are worthy of death, not only do the same, but have pleasure in them that do them." (KJV)

[47] "Know ye not that the unrighteous shall not inherit the kingdom of God? Be not deceived: neither fornicators, nor idolaters, nor adulterers, nor effeminate, nor abusers of themselves with mankind. (KJV)

Ellen on Monday morning (someone Jerry Falwell once called Ellen *Degenerate*). Once again, giving up the anti-gay rhetoric can rightly be marketed as a return to the spirit of the first century church, when Samaritans and Gentiles, Romans and Greeks, women and men, prostitutes and drunks, and the rich and poor were equally welcome among the ranks of the redeemed, when Paul beautifully wrote (Gal. 3.28) that "in Christ" there is "neither Jew nor Gentile, male nor female, slave nor free." CEF churches can simply affirm that the Spirit that leads into all truth (as Jesus taught!) has revealed that in the New Jerusalem there also is neither gay nor straight.

The authors of the March/April 2012 *Foreign Affairs* article ("God and Caesar in America: Why Mixing Religion and Politics is Bad for Both") stress that their data indicate that American Christianity is "feeling the heat from their too close association with partisan politics" and in a "self-correcting tendency" is beginning to pull back (42, 43). Data from their 2011 survey showed a significant drop in church-based political activity: "In 2006, 32 percent of Americans who belonged to a congregation reported hearing sermons with political content 'once every month or two' or 'several times a month.' By 2011, that figure had fallen to 19 percent" (43). The authors claim that these data demonstrate a likelihood that clergy are beginning to sense that Americans still have an "aversion to blurring the lines between God and Caesar" and that clergy have, therefore, "opted to stick with God" (43). We can hope so, but the rise of tea party Republicanism and certain religious personalities give pause.

And what if CEF churches stopped preaching antagonism against science—origins studies particularly? The worn out story of the young congregant who goes away to college and takes his first biology course and spends many sleepless nights thereafter trying to reconcile that with Genesis could be eliminated altogether. Religion *must* drop that which the evidence does not support, without waiting another 100 years to do so. CEF Christianity *must* accommodate the truths of science. The great evolutionary biologist Stephen Jay Gould (1941-2002) had it right—there is a magisterium of science and a magisterium of religion. Science tells us how things work in the natural world and religion tells us a way to find inner peace and joy and "love of neighbor" in that same natural world. The missions of science and religion are not the same. Religion needs to understand that, right away, and stop trampling on the holy ground of science, a losing battle that will only serve to strengthen the case against faith.

Perhaps R1563, a male in his fifties, exemplifies the possibilities. He was raised in a devout liberal/moderate Catholic home. In his late teens, he underwent a period of intense Bible study and converted to conservative evangelicalism. While an active member of a CEF church, he believed the origins story to be accurate—God created the universe and the Earth and all life thereon. In college, where he studied origin science, he was convinced otherwise: he accepted as fact the evolution of life by Darwinian means. This did not, however, weaken his faith or send him careening off an overpass. Why not? Because he had been taught in his childhood Catholic upbringing that "God used nature to create the universe." It was not, therefore, "hard to go back to what the Catholic Church accepted and taught me as a child." Indeed, while he realized that evangelicals were wrong on origins—Genesis was not to be taken literally—he "remained [for many years] an evangelical Bible believer in every other area of faith." Therefore, he claims, "evolution had nothing to do with my deconversion."

CEF churches also need to give up on the circuitous and tortured theologies of theodicy. They need to stop teaching that God is always in control and that God protects his own. While that may be true spiritually speaking or in an ultimate "when we all get to Heaven" sense, it most certainly is not true in the physical realm. Good people die slow and painful deaths every second of every day and bad people enjoy good health until their 100th birthday. Wars happen. Innocent people die. Famine kills millions. Kindergartners get cancer. CEF congregations can still teach that God wants all to be healed and whole but they have to abandon the theology that led Pat Robertson and Jerry Falwell after the 9/11 attacks to blame[48] the attacks on gays, lesbians, feminists, and Planned Parenthood.

Rabbi Harold Kushner, writing in his forty-year-old classic *When Bad Things Happen to Good People* offers a way out. Those who wish to choose faith must accept the overwhelming evidence that God is not in control of everything and that God cannot *right now* heal the world and that God is not, therefore, omnipotent: "The Bible, after all, repeatedly speaks of God as the special protector of the poor, the widow, and the orphan, without raising the question of how it happened that they became poor, widowed, or orphaned in the first place" (Kushner 45). We simply cannot, the Rabbi suggests, "ask God to change the laws of nature for our benefit" (116). Admitting

---

[48] They later apologized.

that sometimes "SHIT HAPPENS" (as the bumper sticker puts it) is not an abandonment of the faith or a diminishing of the doctrine of ultimate spiritual sovereignty of God; it is, instead, accepting reality on reality's terms. After all, Jesus taught that sometimes towers fall on innocent people and that sometimes babies are born blind, all without any spiritual reason.

Alongside the issue of pain and suffering in this life is that of eternal pain and suffering in hellfire. That teaching does not work these days. Mainline Christians, "nones," and of course the secular-minded and agnostic and atheist do not for a moment believe in hellfire and eternal punishment of immortal souls that didn't believe the correct doctrines. Here, too, CEF Christianity can take the high road and re-interpret long-held views about an allegedly just God whose punishment, if eternal hellfire were true, is far in excess of the crimes of one short lifetime. Many Christian denominations have already done so; many more must do so.

Only by stepping away from conservative politics and the politicization of the church and the concomitant rejection of equality for gays, coupled with acceptance of the power of science to discern truth and make the world a better place, and elevation of Jesus as Word of God in place of Bible as Word of God, alongside a new theology of theodicy and judgment can the CEF movement take the high—and moral—ground into the twenty-first century. Doing so will, perhaps, save the faith and the faithful a whole lot of unnecessary heartache and disappointment. If they don't heed the call, their relevancy will diminish with each passing day.

Afterword

The battle between atheism and theism is as ancient as humanity and unlikely to subside as long as the human species, with its unimaginable progeny in the millennia that may lie ahead, is on this old earth or flourishing in colonies on other planets. Who can say that the conflict is not one that divides all thinking creatures on billions of other planets in this monstrous universe of ours? Who can say that it is not a conflict that will last until the end of time? —*Martin Gardner* (3)

Appendix I

Agnostic/Atheist Websites

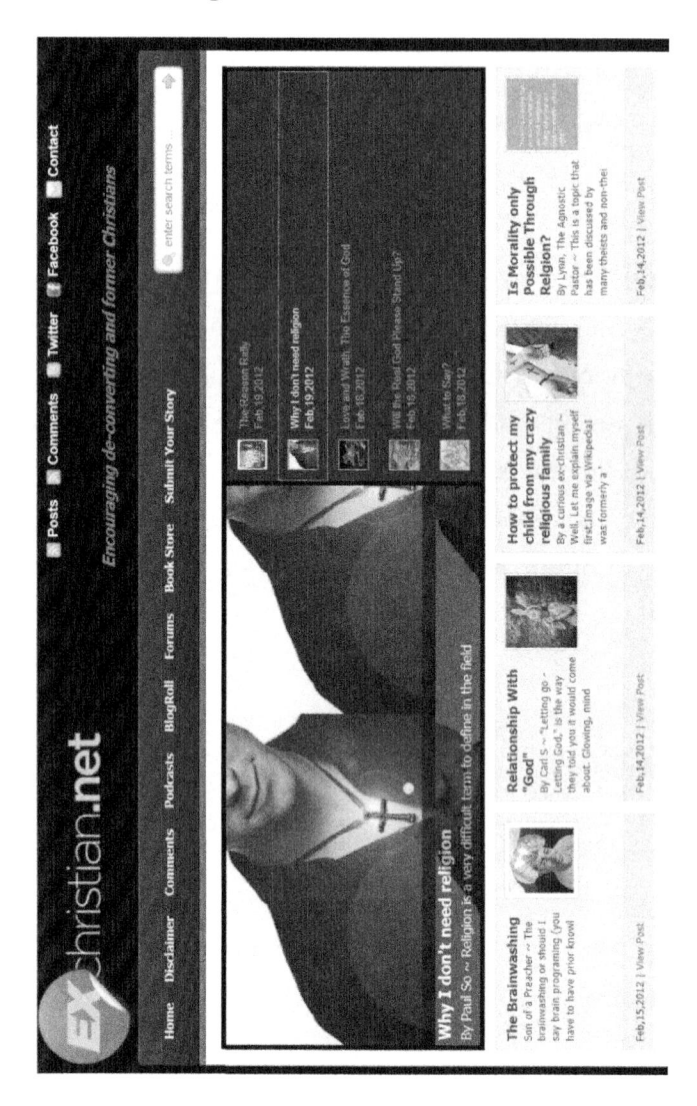

Figure 10: Ex-Christian.Net has been an important gathering place for "deconverting and former Christians" since its founding in April 2005 by former CEF Christian Dave Van Allen. As of mid-2012, Ex-Christian.Net had 6,385 members. Ex-Christian.Net also has a Facebook page, with 3,059 members. Page accessed February 19, 2012. (Gray scaled for print.)

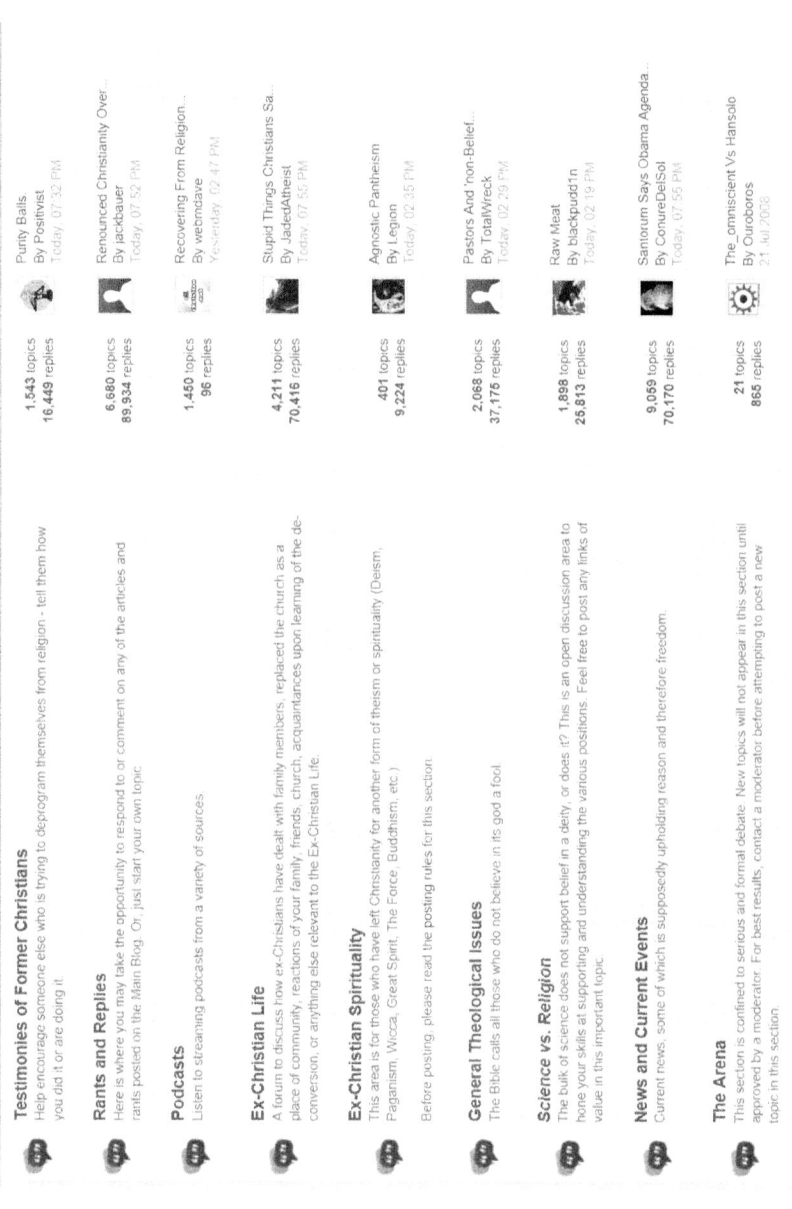

Testimonies of Former Christians
Help encourage someone else who is trying to deprogram themselves from religion - tell them how you did it or are doing it.

1,543 topics
16,449 replies

Purity Balls
By Positivst
Today 07:32 PM

Rants and Replies
Here is where you may take the opportunity to respond to or comment on any of the articles and rants posted on the Main Blog. Or, just start your own topic.

6,680 topics
89,934 replies

Renounced Christianity Over...
By jackbauer
Today 07:52 PM

Podcasts
Listen to streaming podcasts from a variety of sources.

1,450 topics
96 replies

Recovering From Religion...
By webmdave
Yesterday 02:47 PM

Ex-Christian Life
A forum to discuss how ex-Christians have dealt with family members, replaced the church as a place of community, reactions of your family, friends, church, acquaintances upon learning of the de-conversion, or anything else relevant to the Ex-Christian Life.

4,211 topics
70,416 replies

Stupid Things Christians Sa...
By JadedAtheist
Today 07:55 PM

Ex-Christian Spirituality
This area is for those who have left Christianity for another form of theism or spirituality (Deism, Paganism, Wicca, Great Spirit, The Force, Buddhism, etc.)

Before posting, please read the posting rules for this section.

401 topics
9,224 replies

Agnostic Pantheism
By Legion
Today 02:35 PM

General Theological Issues
The Bible calls all those who do not believe in its god a fool.

2,068 topics
37,176 replies

Pastors And 'non-Belief...
By TotalWreck
Today 02:29 PM

Science vs. Religion
The bulk of science does not support belief in a deity, or does it? This is an open discussion area to hone your skills at supporting and understanding the various positions. Feel free to post any links of value in this important topic.

1,898 topics
25,813 replies

Raw Meat
By blackpudd1n
Today 02:19 PM

News and Current Events
Current news, some of which is supposedly upholding reason and therefore freedom.

9,059 topics
70,170 replies

Santorum Says Obama Agenda...
By ConureDelSol
Today 07:56 PM

The Arena
This section is confined to serious and formal debate. New topics will not appear in this section until approved by a moderator. For best results, contact a moderator before attempting to post a new topic in this section.

21 topics
865 replies

The_omniscient Vs Hansolo
By Ouroboros
21 Jul 2008

Figure 11: Ex-Christian.Net forum, accessed February 19, 2012. (Gray scaled for print.)

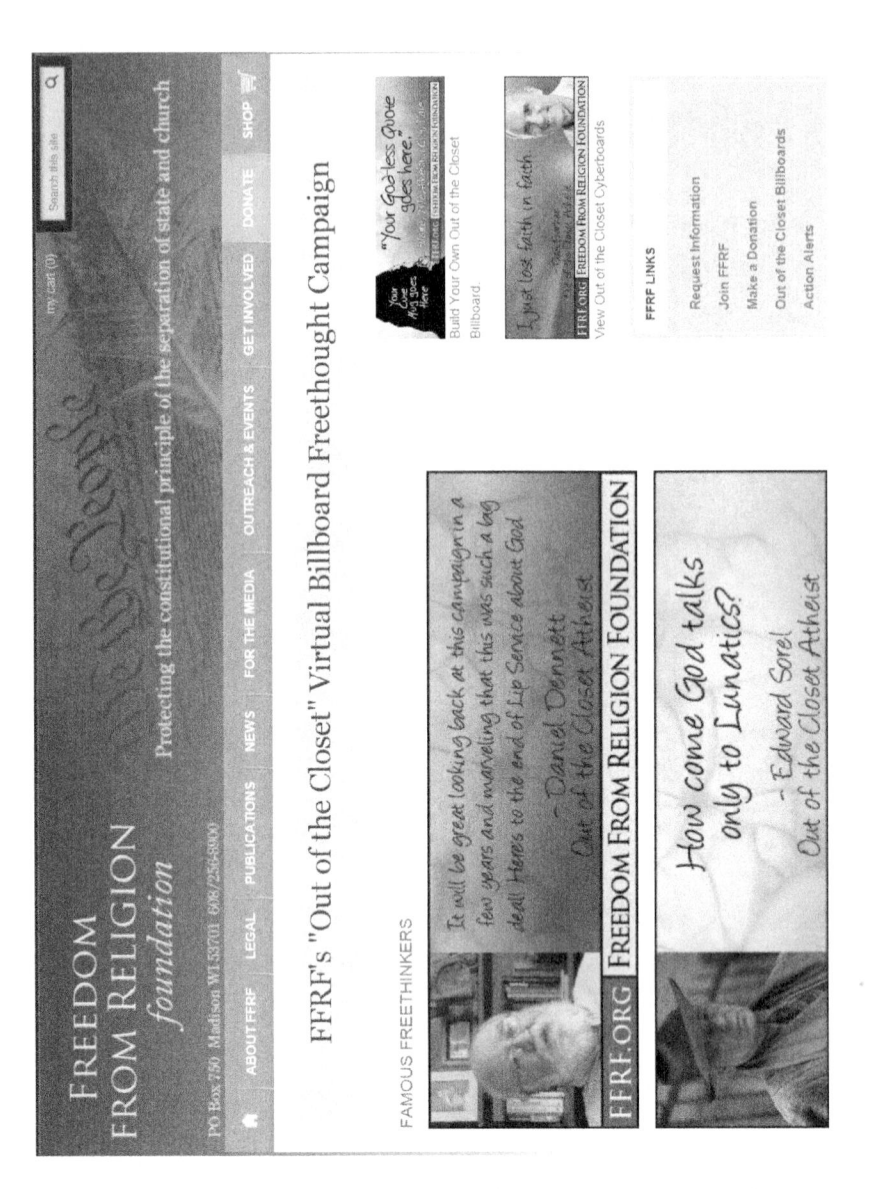

Figure 12: Homepage of the Freedom from Religion Foundation, accessed February 19, 2012. (Gray scaled for print.)

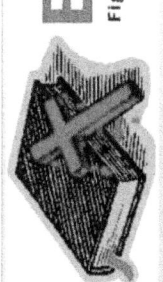

Figure 13: Homepage of EvilBible.com, accessed March 2, 2012. (Gray scaled for print.)

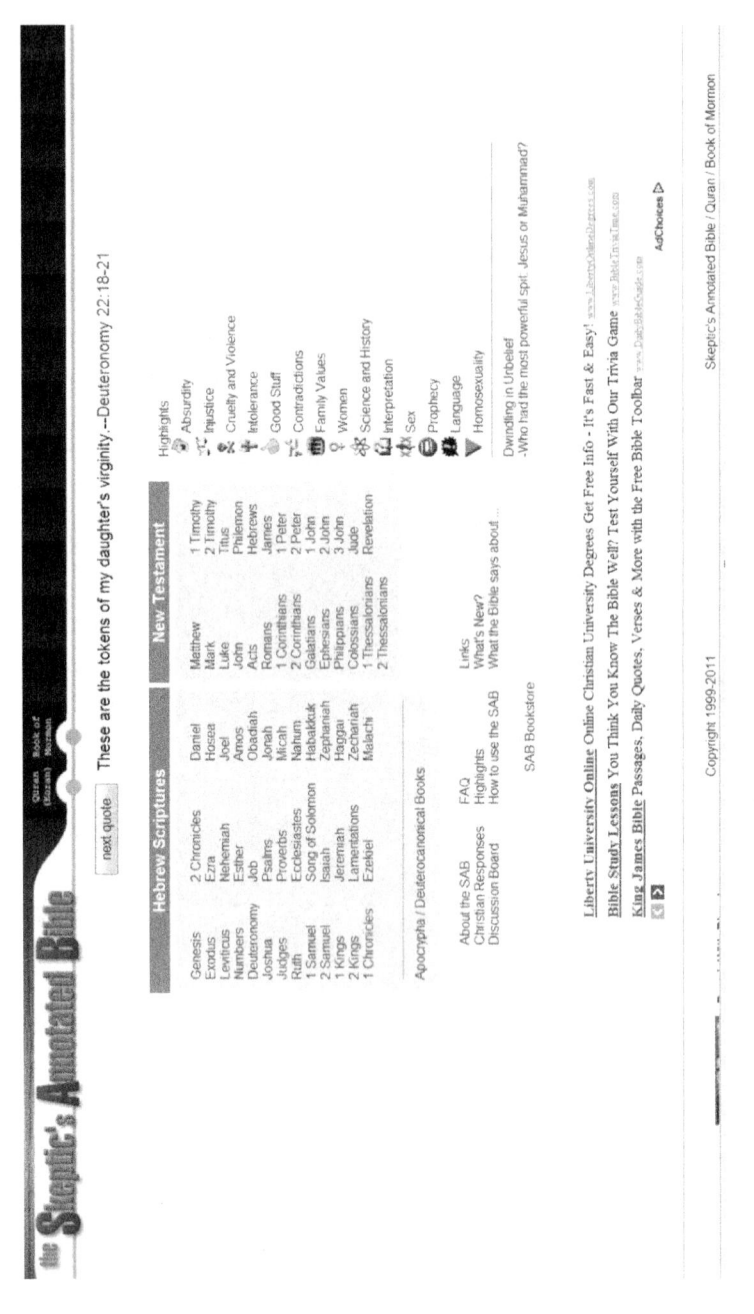

Figure 14: Homepage of SkepticsAnnotatedBible.com, accessed February 19, 2012. (Gray scaled for print.)

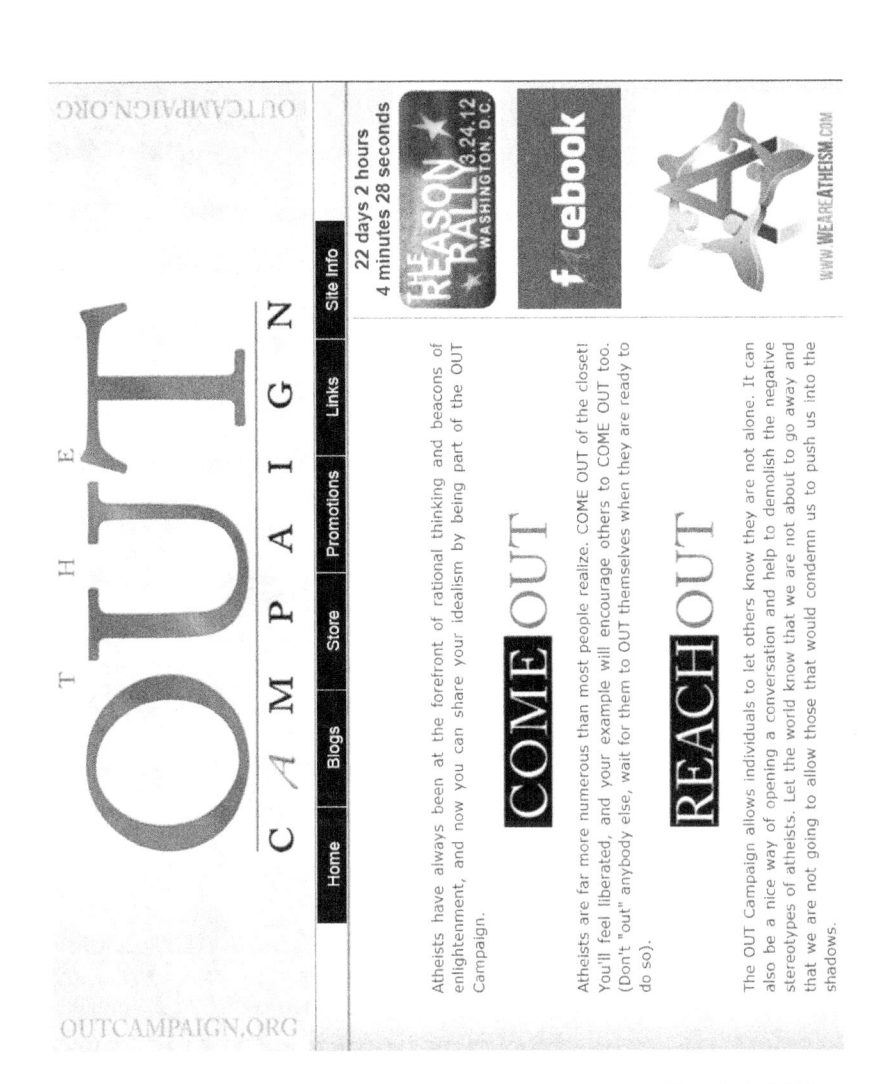

**Figure 15: Homepage of OutCampaign.org, accessed March 1, 2012.
(Gray scaled for print.)**

The Atheist OUT Campaign

Figure 16: Bright red emblem of the Richard Dawkins Foundation's Out Campaign (occasionally used by agnostics / atheists as a Facebook profile picture). (Gray scaled for print.) This image is copyright of its owner(s) (if applicable) and is used solely for historical and scholarly illustrative purposes.

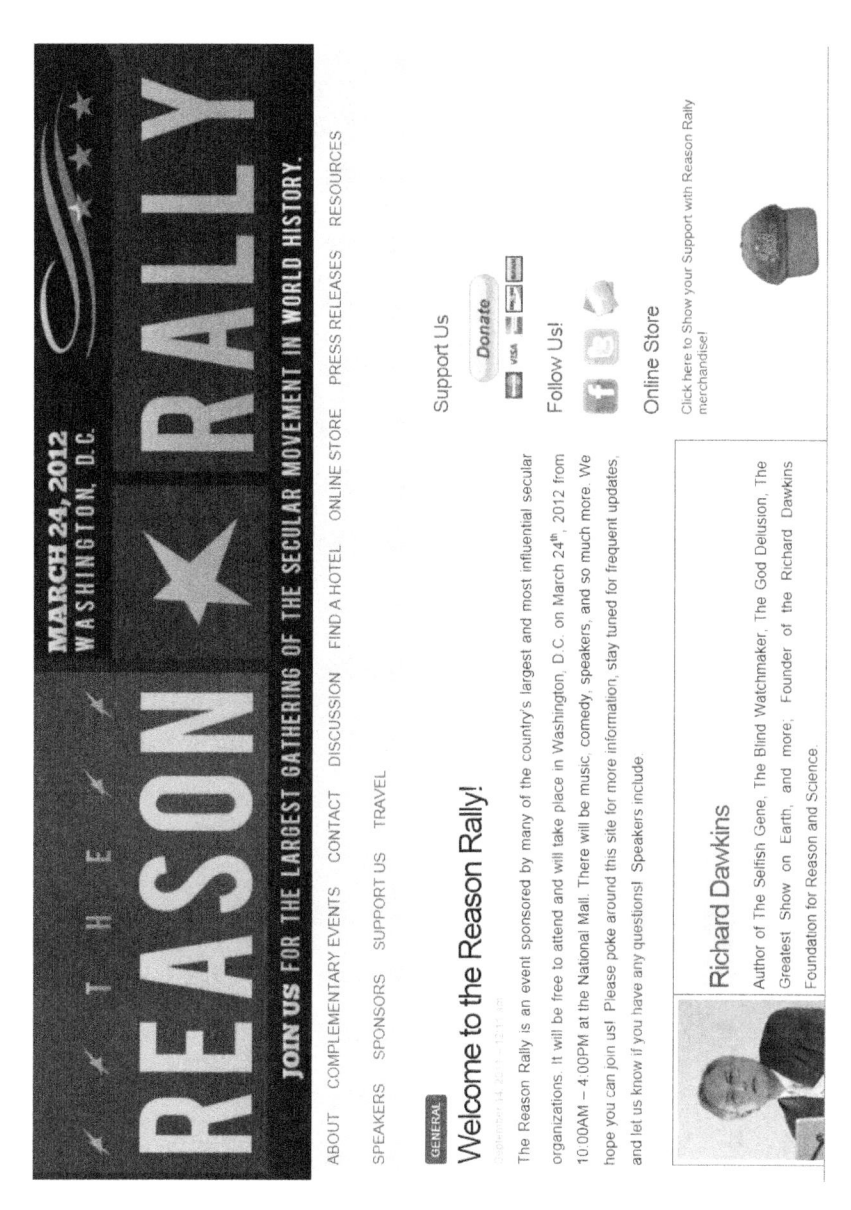

Figure 17: Homepage of The Reason Rally (reasonrally.org), accessed March 2, 2012. (Gray scaled for print.)

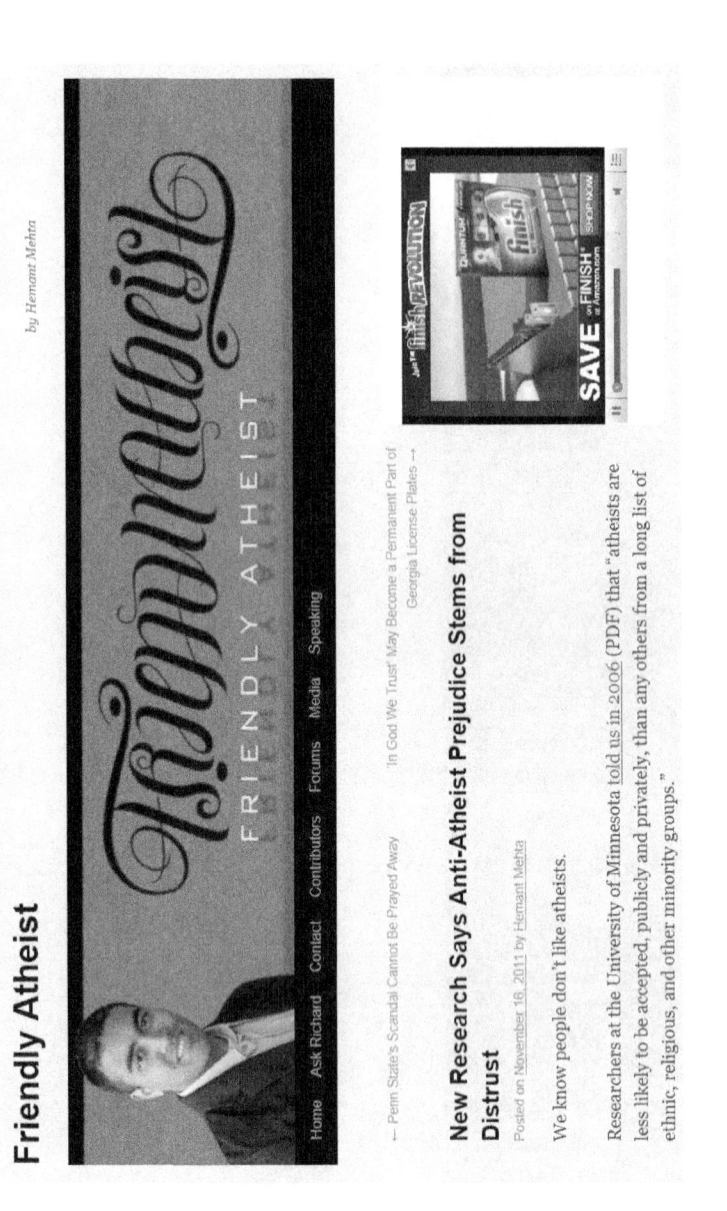

Figure 18: The Friendly Atheist blog
(patheos.com/blogs/friendlyatheist), accessed March 1, 2012. (Gray scaled for print.)

Appendix II

Former Christian Now Agnostic/Atheist (FCNA) Survey

Question 1: How old are you?						
Formerly →	All Respondents Except CEF Christians N=1170	Easter-Christmas Christian, with Some Sunday Schooling N=468	Devout Liberal-Moderate Catholic N=262	Devout Conservative Catholic N=75	Devout Liberal-Moderate Protestant N=365	Devout CEF Protestant N=391
18-29	34.3%	37.6%	32.4%	33.3%	31.5%	28.1%
30-39	30.9%	29.5%	34.0%	34.7%	29.6%	35.8%
40-49	21.2%	20.7%	21.4%	21.3%	21.6%	21.2%
50-59	10.2%	7.9%	9.5%	5.3%	14.5%	10.7%
60-69	2.6%	3.2%	2.7%	2.7%	1.6%	3.8%
70-79	0.9%	0.9%	0.0%	2.7%	1.1%	0.3%
80-89	0.1%	0.2%	0.0%	0.0%	0.0%	0.0%
90+	0.0%	0.0%	0.0%	0.0%	0.0%	0.0%

| **Question 2: Sex** ||||||||
Formerly →	All Respondents Except CEF Christians N=1170	Easter-Christmas Christian, with Some Sunday Schooling N=468	Devout Liberal-Moderate Catholic N=262	Devout Conservative Catholic N=75	Devout Liberal-Moderate Protestant N=365	Devout CEF Protestant N=391
Female	27.2%	27.4%	29.4%	22.7%	26.3%	27.4%
Male	71.7%	72.0%	69.5%	76.0%	72.1%	71.4%
Intersex / Transgender	1.1%	0.6%	1.1%	1.3%	1.6%	1.3%

Question 3: What is your highest level of formal education?

Formerly →	All Respondents Except CEF Christians N=1170	Easter-Christmas Christian, with Some Sunday Schooling N=468	Devout Liberal-Moderate Catholic N=262	Devout Conservative Catholic N=75	Devout Liberal-Moderate Protestant N=365	Devout CEF Protestant N=391
Some high school	1.0%	0.6%	1.1%	2.7%	1.1%	0.8%
High school graduate	4.2%	6.2%	2.7%	4.0%	2.7%	5.4%
Some college	23.6%	25.0%	22.1%	21.3%	23.3%	23.0%
Two-year college degree / certificate	10.1%	10.5%	7.3%	17.3%	10.1%	12.8%
Four-year college degree	27.9%	25.6%	27.9%	24.0%	31.8%	29.4%
Some graduate school	9.4%	9.2%	11.8%	12.0%	7.4%	8.2%
Graduate school degree (master's)	12.2%	11.3%	11.8%	13.3%	13.4%	12.5%
Some post-graduate work	3.1%	4.1%	5.3%	0.0%	0.8%	3.1%
Post-graduate degree (MD, PhD, J.D., etc.)	8.5%	7.5%	9.9%	5.3%	9.3%	4.9%

Question 4: Which type of secondary (high) schooling did you have?						
Formerly →	All Respondents Except CEF Christians N=1170	Easter-Christmas Christian, with Some Sunday Schooling N=468	Devout Liberal-Moderate Catholic N=262	Devout Conservative Catholic N=75	Devout Liberal-Moderate Protestant N=365	Devout CEF Protestant N=391
Public	77.3%	78.8%	65.6%	56.0%	87.9%	83.1%
Home, non-religious	0.9%	0.9%	0.0%	1.3%	1.4%	1.3%
Home, religious	0.8%	0.9%	0.8%	2.7%	0.3%	2.0%
Private, non-religious	4.2%	4.5%	3.8%	8.0%	3.3%	1.8%
Private, religious	16.9%	15.0%	29.8%	32.0%	7.1%	11.8%

Question 5: If you are a two- or four-year college graduate, which type of school did you attend?						
Formerly → (Percent post-secondary graduates in parentheses)	All Respondents Except CEF Christians N=919 (78.5%)	Easter-Christmas Christian, with Some Sunday Schooling N=360 (76.9%)	Devout Liberal-Moderate Catholic N=210 (80.2%)	Devout Conservative Catholic N=57 (76.0%)	Devout Liberal-Moderate Protestant N=292 (80.0%)	Devout CEF Protestant N=391 (77.7%)
Public	75.1%	76.4%	73.8%	71.9%	75.0%	72.4%
Private, non-religious	14.8%	16.4%	16.7%	12.3%	12.0%	10.5%
Private, religious	10.1%	7.2%	9.5%	15.8%	13.0%	17.1%

Question 6: If you have any Bible / religion / divinity degrees, what are they and where (name of school) and when (year of graduation) were they earned?

Twenty-six (26) of 391 former CEF Christians have a degree in religion / Bible / divinity.

Question 7: What was your religious upbringing prior to age 18?						
Formerly →	All Respondents Except CEF Christians N=1170	Easter-Christmas Christian, Some Sunday Schooling N=468	Devout Liberal-Moderate Catholic N=262	Devout Conservative Catholic N=75	Devout Liberal-Moderate Protestant N=365	Devout CEF Protestant N=391
None to very little religious upbringing; my parents were not religious	5.9%	10.5%	2.3%	2.7%	3.3%	4.1%
My parents were not religious, but I was involved in religious groups by my own choice	6.9%	5.3%	5.0%	1.3%	11.5%	7.7%
An Easter – Christmas home, with some Sunday schooling; nothing too intense	28.7%	57.3%	8.8%	2.7%	11.8%	7.2%
Devout liberal / moderate Catholic home	20.6%	10.3%	67.2%	14.7%	1.6%	2.0%
Devout conservative Catholic home	10.1%	3.4%	14.9%	76.0%	1.6%	1.0%
Devout liberal / moderate Protestant home	20.9%	9.4%	1.5%	1.3%	53.7%	4.1%
Devout CEF Protestant home	6.8%	3.8%	0.4%	1.3%	16.4%	73.9%

Question 8: How would you describe your interest in religion prior to age 18?						
Formerly →	All Respondents Except CEF Christians N=1170	Easter-Christmas Christian, with Some Sunday Schooling N=468	Devout Liberal-Moderate Catholic N=262	Devout Conservative Catholic N=75	Devout Liberal-Moderate Protestant N=365	Devout CEF Protestant N=391
Not at all interested	12.1%	19.4%	10.7%	9.3%	4.1%	6.1%
A little interested	29.7%	45.3%	22.5%	12.0%	18.4%	12.0%
Moderate interest	34.4%	28.2%	42.0%	28.0%	38.1%	22.3%
Very interested in religion	23.9%	7.1%	24.8%	50.7%	39.5%	59.6%

Question 8 (responses by sexual orientation): How would you describe your interest in religion prior to age 18?

	Asexual N=16	Exclusively Heterosexual N=1024	Primarily Heterosexual N=325	Bisexual N=97	Primarily homosexual N=35	Exclusively homosexual N=64
Not at all interested	12.5%	11.4%	8.9%	10.3%	5.7%	7.8%
A little interested	37.5%	26.5%	23.7%	20.6%	17.1%	21.9%
Moderate interest	12.5%	32.7%	31.7%	21.6%	34.3%	25.0%
Very interested in religion	37.5%	29.4%	35.7%	47.4%	42.9%	45.3%

Question 9: Some individuals are born into a religion, others have a conversation experience. Please describe how/when/under what circumstances you became a member of the Christian religion. Feel free to provide as much detail as you wish.

Selected Responses[49] of Respondents Identifying as Formerly Conservative / Evangelical / Fundamentalist Protestant (391 of 391 submitted a written response):

Born a liberal Catholic, and had a strong belief in God. I was "born again" in my late teens through intense Bible studies with fundamentalist/evangelical ministers, who converted me from liberal Catholic to conservative Evangelicalism.

§

I was raised Catholic until age 12 with only a moderate family emphasis on religion. At that point my mother was "born again" and became very active in the Assemblies of God, and I was swept along with the tide.

§

At 15yrs I read a Christian end times prophecy book that frightened me into conversion. I was a devout fundamentalist Christian for 25yrs after that.

§

My dad is an evangelical pastor & missionary with a doctorate in divinity. I was barely two years old when I memorized my first bible verse. I only had Christian friends & didn't really realize that was abnormal until late in my high school career.

§

I was born into a conservative (Church of England) protestant

---

[49] Represented here are thirteen of fifty (13 of 50) pages of responses submitted in the FCNA Survey. None of these submissions is cited in the text of the paper. Printed here as submitted.

Christian family. I then became a born again evangelical Christian at age 15.

§

Age 10 I watched a Billy Graham crusade that was televised and wrote a letter to Jesus but did not get saved until age 23. I was in college. Laden with sexual sin from my first and now (only) love...had abortion and sought forgiveness. Felt acceptance and belonging.

§

I was flirted into it.

§

Totally indoctrinated--church three times a week until aged twelve or so then weekly Bible study at home.

§

Born into it, "accepted Christ" at about age 7.

§

had the standard, "God loves you and has a wonderful plan for your life . . ." approach. I think the Vacation Bible School teacher used what was commonly called in my Baptist circles the "Roman Road" set of scriptures to "witness" to me. I converted, was Baptized and was active in youth groups, choirs and other standard worship and study formats. This was in the mid 1970's when I was 14.

§

At age six, I accepted Jesus as my savior at a Jimmy Swaggart revival.

§

Born into it.

§

I felt "convicted" during a sermon at age 13, which I was told was the "age of accountability," so I "got saved." I really meant it, though.

§

I was raised in a very conservative Catholic turned evangelical household. I always considered myself a Christian. It was a very polarized church - we are right, everyone else is wrong. I was raised to "hate the sins love the sinner" but then hate the sinner when they didn't follow our Christian ways. My best friend died when I was 16 and I became "born again" at his funeral. I got baptized later that year.

§

Born into Assemblies of God in 1975 when the televangelism boom was picking up steam. My mother was raised Catholic. My father Methodist. Both joined Assemblies of God after watching the PTL Club in 1974.

§

Born into it. Had multiple occasions of making commitments/dedications or having experiences/moments of increased devotion. I consciously chose to become a follower of Jesus in high school. I read the Bible daily, prayed, fasted, taught the Bible to other people. I wanted to be a minister and dedicated my life to pursuing what I thought was "God's will."

§

Born into probably the most conservative religious family in America. Learned rigid components of Hyper-Calvinism since birth.

§

Moved to a new community when I was 9. A Baptist preacher and his family were right across the street. They were welcoming -- and my own home was not -- so I started going to their church. I got really involved in it and attended Sunday School, Training Union, Girls Auxiliary and Vacation Bible School. I was baptized when I was 10 or 11. Several of my siblings made fun of me for it. My parents did not attend church at all.

§

My parents divorced when I was seven. I started spending more time with my great-grandmother, who took me to a Pentecostal church on every occasion. I remember becoming scared of death and Hell. I don't remember exactly when I became a Christian, but it was around this time. My parents were more lax about religion at the time.

§

I had my own fear-based conversion by age 12 (thanks to the out-of-date "end times" movies that youth group would show).

§

Born into it. Raised Southern Baptist.

§

I was born into an LDS family, 6th generation.

§

From about age six or so I know the whole family went to church every Sunday morning, Sunday night, and midweek Bible Study. By about 12 or 13 I grew scared of going to hell, so I asked to be baptized ("essential for the forgiveness of sins" in my church's tradition and interpretation of, e.g., Acts 2:38). Given substantial personal Bible study over following years, at about 17-18, I decided that wasn't a meaningful conversion, so I asked to be baptized again, now "knowing what I was doing."

§

My parents were moderately religious (Lutheran) up until the early 70's, at which point they became swept up in the "Jesus movement". The pastor of their Lutheran church at the time left, took about half of the congregation with him, including my parents, and started a "non-denominational" fundamentalist church (as I like to say, "holy roller") in the same town. I was about five when this happened, and so I was taken along for the ride and continued to buy into it until I was about 20.

§

I was born into the basic ideas of god, Jesus, etc. but my family was more of an Easter & Christmas family until at the age of

13 our family joined a Pentecostal church. It was all downhill from there.

§

I guess I was born into religion. Until I was 6 or 7, my parents were occasional Protestants (occasional Sundays, holidays). But then my father went through some personal turmoil and was saved at a Church of God revival. He came home and tearfully shared the news with the rest of us. We then became a devout, fundamentalist family. From then on we attended the Pentecostal church at least once per week. My parents were evangelical and spoke in tongues. We eventually moved over to an Assembly of God church. And, at one point, my father was the CFO of Benny Hinn's mega church. I would say that I always felt uncomfortable at these churches. I was coerced into "getting saved" when I was about 8 or 9. I was very curious about religion throughout my childhood and teenage years. I doubted the truth of the preaching at my church, but was too scared to be a non-believer as my parents (father especially) were serious millennialists.

§

"Baptized" when I was 12 years old. At the time was consumed with fear of hell/death, and wanted to make sure I was saved.

§

My family comes from a long line of So. Baptist ministers, going back to at least the Revolutionary War in America, Britain prior to that. I was baptized into the Baptist denomination at age 7. And was a Christian fundamentalist for over 45 years before deconverting.

§

I devoted myself to Christianity after a bad personal experience. I suffer from bi-polar disorder and paranoia, and I found the church helped me feel better about myself. It did not help me in that I stopped taking my medications because I believe Jesus had healed me, and being bi-polar and paranoid while attending an eschatologically minded fundamentalist church is not really what could be called healthy.

§

I had a typical evangelical conversion at the age of 12 when I asked Jesus to forgive my sins and enter into my heart. I was on my own at the time, but it was the result of many years of having the gospel preached at our church.

§

Although I was always churches, we were expected to have an experience of being saved, which I did at a youth group function at 16. I wanted it desperately, so I convinced myself it was real. Of course the music and so forth helped.

§

At 25 I went to Evangelical churches with my protestant wife. I got very involved, and began teaching bible studies, and Sunday school.

§

At 16 I had a born again experience - or so I thought - after a Christian rock band played in a local venue. My Christian vigour lasted for ten years, while I was active in my church. Things tapered off after that.

§

I was raised Southern Baptist and left the church at 15 when I became disenfranchised with the fire and brimstone ideology of my church leaders. After that, I read the Bible in search of spiritual understanding and was converted to the Church of Jesus Christ of Latter-Day Saints by a group of close friends. I was young, confused and searching for a deeper level of understanding out of life and the church appealed with an easy answer to all of those questions. I prayed, and my desire manifested itself in the form of the placebo effect, making me sincerely believe that I was touched by the Holy Ghost. After that moment, I became a devout Mormon.

§

I was taught it from a very young age. I never had a conversion experience, or any real emotional experience for that matter. I did stubbornly defend my position at the time, but I think I did so more from the standpoint of wanting to be right, or possibly being afraid of death and hell than anything else. I always thought something was wrong with me since I obviously wasn't feeling anything/hearing god. I did have two formal baptisms. The first when I was 10 and the second when I was 16. The first was at a vacation bible school program in the summer and I only did it because a friend did. The second was to impress a girl in the church, lol. Hope this helps.

§

Was born Baptist, but became committed around 13. Remained with Baptist church until age 25, then attended a United Pentecostal church with a friend. Became highly religious, was baptized, wanted to enter ministry.

§

I have an extreme personality as it is, so even though my mom wasn't very religious, I went with it full force. She never really hindered my efforts, but my dad (who I didn't live with) was (and still is) a hugely conservative evangelical fundamentalist, so he really appreciated my devotion.

§

I had my first "conversion" at the age of 4. My mother had read a scary children's story to me about hell and the last days.

§

I was born into an evangelical family who was actively involved in Christian Ministry and later were faculty at a Bible College.

§

I was not born into a religious home, but my father started meeting with a pastor when I was 6. I eaves dropped on their conversations from my bedroom and said the "sinners prayer".

My parents converted and our house was fundamentalist from that point on.

§

I was born into a traditional southern family. Jesus was always lurking around corners and spying over shoulders... Following the church wasn't a choice it was expected of me.

§

Brought up protestant, but my parents strongly believe in conversion experiences. I had about twenty-seven of them but could never convince myself I was "saved."

§

I was born into religion to very devout parents. I was lukewarm religious until I had a near-death experience at age 14. For several years after that, believing I was at once punished by the incident and also given a second chance, I became more intensely devout.

§

Born/brainwashed into it. My faith was strong. Was youth leader and role model in church, led many to Christ.

§

I grew up in the rural Bible belt, where Christianity and the literal truth of the Bible are simply an axiomatic part of the culture. Although my parents themselves were not especially observant and did not attend church, they were nominally theistic at least insofar as teaching me to believe in the Christian God and sending me to a few summer Bible classes. Growing up I came to believe that if Christianity were true, it should be a more important part of life than my parents treated it, and so when I left home for college I sought out religious groups during my freshman year and became deeply involved for the next three or so years, until I eventually reasoned my way out of those beliefs.

§

At age 35 I became involved with an independent, fundamental, bible believing Baptist church after attending a revival meeting with a friend I admired. I followed along when she led me in the prayer for salvation, and I began attending services. I went to Sunday school, Wednesday night bible study, Tuesday morning ladies bible study and soul-winning (door knocking) on Saturdays. This was a large church with a very charismatic pastor and they were very good at making new members feel important and special.

§

I was born into a religious environment (small town southeastern US), and was taught religious concepts as though they were general facts starting at pre-school age. I naturally believed these at such a young age the same way I believed other unquestioned "facts" that I was taught by trusted adults. I did not encounter secular views until adolescence. The fact that my parents were only moderately religious made the experience more tolerable than it was for many of my friends, who had excessively religious parents. This, coupled with the fact that more positive aspects of the religion were emphasized (forgiveness, heaven, etc.) made me less inclined to question or rebel against the beliefs until much later (late teens- I am now 29).

§

I was born into a fundamentalist Christian family (my parents were students at Bob Jones University, and I was born at the school's hospital and grew up hearing how Bob Jones himself held me as an infant.) However, my family did not believe that you were "born" a Christian; one had to be "born again" and I had such an experience at a young age (I do not remember exactly when).

§

I grew up in a very Christian home, and was surrounded by talk of Jesus at all times. I think I was five when I prayed to be saved. We were always very active in the church, I didn't have any idea what life without church could be like.

§

I was born into a family that was very religious. I often went to church 3 times a week, sometimes more. My conversion came at about 16 after many fire and brimstone sermons and hours and hours of Bible classes and chapel services at school. After that, I became much more interested in religion and even taught a children's group for awhile.

§

I was raised attending the Church of Christ, attendance (twice on Sunday and Wednesday was the norm) was expected and being baptized also. By 14 or 15 I was pretty sure I was an atheist as I simply could not wrap my head around the religious crap anymore. It simply did not make sense and all the pains everyone took to try and explain how it was real just became comical. Also, I found the claims of "miracles" rather insulting (God answered my prayer for a raise but ignores all the pleas of people being murdered, starved, facing natural disasters?) and the response at every funeral, regardless of the age or reason of the deceased, always pissed me off - "God decided it was time for them to come home." Ugh!

§

One grandmother often spoke of the afterlife and the coming apocalypse that would soon hit the Earth. It was a dark, bleak message to give to a teen.

§

Prayed the "Sinner's Prayer" at age six at a summer Vacation Bible School. I had been raised in the church my entire life, but this was probably the first proselytizing event that I was mentally capable of understanding, awake for, and paying attention to.

§

I was converted to Evangelicalism from a previously agnostic belief system when I was 19, after a very difficult first year and a half of college. I had been sexually assaulted by a friend, and was having a very rough time. I was depressed and failing all of my classes, and had started drinking heavily. My former roommate was a member of Campus Crusade for Christ, and when I returned to school after a semester off, I went to a meeting they were having to see what it was all about. I had been invited before by my old roommate and a staff member, and when I got there, the staff member (Erin) remembered me. She latched on to me, and "led me to Christ"--in a Wendy's. Soon after I started attending church regularly, going to two or three bible studies a week. When I came home after school still wasn't going well for me, I became more involved with a large "mega" Evangelical church.

§

I converted in a Christian camp. Involved very little sleep and social pressure.

§

Was coming off drugs and living on the street. They showed kindness when others didn't, so I gave it a go, but this was kind of a condition of their friendship, they badger you. But then I was drawn in and started to believe. Had always believed in God but started to believe in the Pentecostal version.

§

I grew up in an extremely religious household. Church every Sunday was mandatory, and my family had their own Bible Study a few times a week. When I was 16, after meeting my girlfriend (now wife), I converted with her family to Messianic Judaism, an evangelical branch of Christianity that is externally Jewish, but internally Christian.

§

My first girlfriend of a couple years dumped me at 16 years of age. Obviously my world crumbled, I felt unloved, and the unconditional love of Jesus was incredibly appealing and I was attracted to the promises of love and acceptance made to me by a local youth pastor and various members of the Pentecostal church he belonged to. I made a lot of friends and found the acceptance I had been craving.

§

I was raised in a religious home with no other alternatives ever presented to me. I went to church, Sunday school, bible camp, and vacation bible school. At age 10 I accepted Jesus as my personal savior and was baptized in my church. At this point in my life my entire religious education was given to me by my church. I wouldn't say I had a "conversion", any more than I "converted" from elementary school to middle school. My decision was just a natural progression of what was expected of me by my church and family.

§

Conversion at a charismatic church targeting young people

§

Born into religion in a small, conservative town in SW Michigan. The fear of god was drummed into me very early. Was baptized out of fear of going to hell rather than devotion to faith.

§

I was dragged to church every week

§

I found religion when I had a mystical experience that to this very day I cannot explain logically. This experience led me to believe that Christianity was the only truth and everyone who didn't believe in Christ as their lord and savior would be damned. However, as time passed, I couldn't avoid this experience and the meanings that resulted from it kept contradicting my religion. After awhile, I finally decided to disregard the belief that God was bound to one specific religion and the rest were of the devil. Now I live according to my own beliefs, which are unaffiliated to any specific dogma. I believe that if God were to exist, then he or she would love me no matter what because I was created by them to be who I am. If God doesn't exist, it doesn't matter anyways.

§

Being in a fundamentalist Baptist household, they scared you often with hell, so they'd have you say the "sinner's prayer". Then you would be "saved". Still leaving of course in your mind the nagging feeling that you didn't mean it enough. A culture of fear really.

§

My mother had a very fundamentalist belief system and she took us faithfully to church 3x/ week plus extra church activities. Bible readings were mandatory daily. I was baptized into that religion as a teenager. While I had been trained to believe that that was a conversion experience, it was really the culmination of years of brainwashing to get me to that point. My worldview was framed with a mistrust of science and a belief in the literal interpretation of the Bible.

§

I became religious when I was at the age of 5 or 6. It also coincided with the time I was being home-schooled. My mother was deeply religious, and she was very controlling of what I watched and what I learned when I was home-schooled.

§

I was five years old and taken to an Easter mega church production which reproduce a theatrical "passion of the Christ" style show. I was so upset and afraid of hell that I officially "said the prayer" that night. I was in church every Sunday and Wednesday since I was born.

§

My entire family is devout Christian, and my parents met in seminary. My father is a pastor, so I spent my whole life being

surrounded by religion and church. I never had a choice in my beliefs, but it took me until college to realize that.
§
I was born into a Pentecostal family, and attended two "Jesus" camps a summer from the time I was 12 until I was 18
§
Married a fundamentalist.

Question 10[50]: When you were Christian (before the conversion process commenced), would you describe yourself as:

Formerly →	All Respondents Except CEF Christians N=1170	Easter-Christmas Christian, with Some Sunday Schooling N=468	Devout Liberal-Moderate Catholic N=262	Devout Conservative Catholic N=75	Devout Liberal-Moderate Protestant N=365	Devout CEF Protestant N=391
An Easter – Christmas Christian, with occasional Sunday schooling	40.0%	100%	0.0%	0.0%	0.0%	0.0%
A devout liberal / moderate Catholic	22.4%	0%	100%	0.0%	0.0%	0.0%
A devout conservative Catholic Christian	6.4%	0%	0.0%	100%	0.0%	0.0%
A devout liberal / moderate Protestant	31.2%	0%	0.0%	0.0%	100%	0.0%
A devout conservative evangelical / fundamentalist Protestant	0.0%	0%	0.0%	0.0%	0.0%	100%

[50] This is the question that was used to subdivide by type the 1,561 former Christians who responded to the online survey, thus the diagonal (left to right, top to bottom) 100% within each of the 2nd-6th columns/categories.

Question 11: If you were a Protestant Christian, which denomination were you affiliated with?

Formerly →	All Respondents Except CEF Christians N=498	Easter-Christmas Christian, with Some Sunday Schooling N=204	Devout Liberal-Moderate Catholic N=12	Devout Conservative Catholic N=6	Devout Liberal-Moderate Protestant N=276	Devout CEF Protestant N=386
Liberal / moderate Baptist	12.0%	12.3%	41.7% (5)	16.7% (1)	10.5%	5
Conservative Baptist	10.8%	8.8%	25.0% (3)	50% (3)	10.9%	82
Liberal / moderate Methodist	16.3%	21.1%	8.3% (1)	16.7% (1)	13.0%	2
Conservative Methodist	3.8%	6.4%	0.0%	0.0%	2.2%	13
Lib / moderate Pentecostal / Charismatic	3.0%	1.5%	0.0%	0.0%	4.3%	4
Conservative Pentecostal / Charismatic	3.0%	2.9%	0.0%	0.0%	3.3%	63
Liberal / moderate Presbyterian	11.4%	12.7%	8.3% (1)	0.0%	10.9%	0.0%
Conservative Presbyterian	2.4%	1.0%	0.0%	0.0%	3.6%	13
Liberal / moderate Lutheran	18.1%	20.6%	0.0%	16.7% (1)	17.0%	1
Conservative Lutheran	3.1%	3.9%	0.0%	0.0%	3.6%	16
Lib / moderate Episcopal	6.8%	4.9%	8.3% (1)	0.0%	8.3%	1
Conservative Episcopal	2.0%	2.0%	0.0%	0.0%	2.2%	2
Latter-day Saint	5.4%	1.5%	8.3% (1)	0.0%	8.3%	28
Jehovah's Witness	1.2%	0.5%	0.0%	0.0%	1.8%	17

Note on Question 11: 139 individuals chose "other" and listed denominations that they felt did not easily fit within these categories, such as Worldwide Church of God (Herbert W. Armstrong), Seventh-Day Adventist, and Church of Christ. In addition, 18 who had formerly identified as Catholic answered this question, thus slightly skewing the data (these responses are noted above in parentheses).

Question 12: When you were Christian (before the deconversion process commenced), what did you believe about the Bible?						
Formerly →	All Respondents Except CEF Christians N=1170	Easter-Christmas Christian, with Some Sunday Schooling N=468	Devout Liberal-Moderate Catholic N=262	Devout Conservative Catholic N=75	Devout Liberal-Moderate Protestant N=365	Devout CEF Protestant N=391
It was the infallible, inerrant Word of God (fundamentalist)	5.6%	4.7%	2.3%	10.7%	8.2%	58.6%
It was the Word of God, written by men under divine inspiration	66.6%	55.1%	72.9%	76.0%	74.8%	38.4%
It was a significant cultural document, mixing human wisdom and error, some history and some legend, but by no means of supernatural / divine origin	23.5%	33.3%	20.6%	10.7%	15.6%	2.0%
It was a book no more special than any other of antiquity	4.3%	6.8%	4.2%	2.7%	1.4%	1.0%

Question 13: How would you describe your views about the Bible now?							
Formerly →	All Respondents Except CEF Christians N=1170	Easter-Christmas Christian, with Some Sunday Schooling N=468	Devout Liberal-Moderate Catholic N=262	Devout Conservative Catholic N=75	Devout Liberal-Moderate Protestant N=365	Devout CEF Protestant N=391
It is the infallible, inerrant Word of God (fundamentalist)	0.1%	0.0%	0.0%	0.0%	0.3%	0.0%
It is the Word of God, written by men under divine inspiration	0.4%	0.2%	0.4%	1.3%	0.5%	1.0%
It is a significant cultural document, mixing human wisdom and error, some history and some legend, but by no means of supernatural / divine origin	53.1%	49.4%	54.6%	48.0%	57.8%	55.2%
It is a book no more special than any other of antiquity	46.4%	50.4%	45.0%	50.7%	41.4%	43.7%

Question 14. If your views of the Bible changed during your years as a Christian and leading up to your deconversion, what was the impetus for that change, how difficult was that change, over how long a period did the change occur, and what did you end up believing about the Bible? Please use as much space as you wish.

Selected Responses[51] of Respondents Identifying as Formerly Conservative / Evangelical / Fundamentalist Protestant (330 of 391 submitted a written response):

Life experiences showed the Bible to be fallible and dead wrong (cynical) about human nature…The God of the Bible is represented as being immoral and accepting of the most cruel acts. It took over 10 years for me to learn this the hard way. If a God exists, it isn't the one written about in the Bible.

§

My deconversion lasted over a period of about seven years. It was very, very difficult, especially the first stages because the "sin" of questioning my beliefs and the bible was a nearly insurmountable obstacle. Ultimately I concluded that the Old Testament was the mythology of an ancient people, and the New Testament was the literature of an emerging cult, shaped in part by internal conflicts, agendas, infighting, and corruption. My views continued to shape long after my actual deconversion.

§

My views changed when I finally investigated for myself. I saw the errors and contradictions and that led to a rejection of inerrancy but I was still a Christian. Learning more about

---

[51] Represented here are eighteen of ninety-seven (18 of 97) pages submitted in the FCNA Survey. Submissions in **bold** were cited, in whole or in part, in the text of the paper. Printed here as submitted.

science, astronomy, geology, anthropology, etc., led to my eventual rejection of religion and theism.

§

My changing view of the bible was a major factor in my deconversion. I had what I believed was a close and personal relationship with god. Still, I knew even as a kid that people fool themselves about many things. The bible was the foundation of what I considered evidence for god's existence and all of the other premises of Christianity. There were a few other things about the bible that didn't seem consistent or didn't seem to add up, though I can't remember specifically what my questions were then.

§

There was a gradual transition from believing it was the infallible word of god, to believing it was divinely inspired, to eventually discovering it was nothing but myth and legend.

§

When I was a teenager, I started to question why my friends of other or no faith were going to hell just due to an accident of birth and it grew from there over several years.

§

As a Catholic I was never required to read the Bible. But I did start to read the Bible when I became a Protestant Christian. At first I found the Bible interesting and read it daily. Eventually I started to question the infallibility of the Bible. This of course caused some trouble with the elders of the church. I also became aware how much of the Bible depicted women as inferior to men. I had seen this in Catholicism too. As a mother of two young daughters this view of women in the eyes of religion started to make me doubtful of a loving and perfect God. Though I remained in the congregation for a few more years. My belief in God was already crumbling.

§

When I deconverted I stopped believing in what was written in the bible.

§

The more I studied the Bible, its history, and other literature as an English major in college, the less clear it became to me that it was "divine" just because "God said so."

§

as i began thinking more independently i saw more and more errors and logical/moral flaws in the bible, and have ended up seeing it as another incorrect religious text which is very dangerous when believed in fully

§

Reading the Bible through in a year is what led to my de-conversion.

§

Took a Geology class and finally realized that the Earth and the Universe is older than what is described in the Bible. I thought, if they were wrong about something as important as that, what else could they be wrong about?

§

The impetus for the change was that the typical creationist timeline did not match what science tells us.... The change was very painful emotionally and continues today.

§

Once I learned the principles of logic then studying the Bible led to my de-conversion.

§

I have something I wrote to explain the whole process to people if you'd like me to include it. Basically, I was very serious about the Bible, I was a music minister, I went on many mission trips, etc. On the mission trips in particular I started to notice that people didn't seem to be as much "in darkness" as I had been taught... they seemed like normal people who were trying to find meaning in their lives just like I was. And many of them were quite happy. The concept of "hell" always bothered me too, and I began to ask some serious questions about it when I was around age 25. Those questions led to more questions.

§

Honestly, what made me change my views was simply reading the Bible! Now, I believe it is a document that is very much a product of its culture and time period, like the Epic of Gilgamesh or any other ancient/old document. I think it was created by humans (men, to be precise), and was in no way influenced by any god.

§

Impetus was research and educating myself. Extremely difficult, earthshaking, to learn my religion was a fraud. Months to know it was a fraud. Years to learn all the details. Bible is passed down mythology, and not "truth".

§

I'll sum it up with: Science is able to back up its assertions with evidence. The Bible could never do so.

§

It started with small questions/observations....The biggest part of the change happened over a 2-year period after my first college degree, when I had lots of time to study on my own. It was VERY difficult at first, b/c I was so afraid of offending God by doubting, but I was compelled to pursue the truth. I ended up seeing the Bible and written by fallible humans, and quite on par with other ancient religious and mythic literature.

§

I believed the Bible could be shown to be factually correct. My attempts to demonstrate that led me to discover the many errors in it.

§

This was a very difficult transition, it took at least a decade to become comfortable with the thought that everything I

believed as a child was a lie, and I was not in fact "turning my back on God."

§

I started to have doubts about the infallibility. Then over the years I did other reading and heard other people speak and slowly I started to harbor really serious doubts. Took quite a few years though till I could admit to myself I didn't believe anymore

§

I sat down and read the Bible from cover to cover out of genuine interest and the desire for something more. Little-by-little it became impossible for me to believe in the mythology I was raised with. I progressed from Biblical literalism to a more liberal interpretation and settled into viewing the Bible as mostly erroneous and largely immoral. This took several years. The conflict between Evangelic Christianity and modern science (biology and physics in particular) as well as the various social conflicts (bigotry towards homosexuals) provided a catalyst and the Internet was very helpful finding information.

§

I accepted that the Problem of Evil was insolvable, hence YHWH couldn't exist, hence the scriptures were written by primitive bigoted desert dwellers. All the apologetics I used to think made perfect sense blew over like a house of cards. The Bible may be flourished with beautiful, historically significant literature, and I can always appreciate that, but the hatred, hell doctrine, etc. wasn't hard to let go of by any stretch. I couldn't be happier that it isn't true.

§

Harder and harder to believe in the Bible Hell. Then started reading about all the self-contradictory passages in the Bible. Took about 3 years, at age 59-62

§

My views began shifting later in high school when I saw such religious disagreement even among Christians. The gradual process was aided by attending a New Testament class in college in which the professor -- a pastor himself -- taught about historical criticism of the Bible and understanding it within its own context as well as peeling back the layers to learn the historical truth to what happened. Throughout my journey I have read a number of books my Bart Ehrman, Michael Shermer and Elaine Pagels.

§

Studying religions at a university helped me sort through my beliefs and I came to see all religions as equal. Equally wrong, equally harmful, equally misleading.

§

As I child, I had an engineering bent. I laid out the lines of Noah's Ark (measurements provided in the Bible). It became obvious to me at about 10 years old that this vessel could not have carried said cargo. That was the end of my belief in the inerrancy of the Bible.

§

Inconsistency between the Old and New Testaments were always a source of confusion. Taking advanced bible classes in college made this imbalance more acute. Scientific study and understanding of geologic time and biologic evolution certainly played a role. Knowledge of books such as the "lost" gospels and biblical apocrypha raised a lot of questions. But, the most significant impact was made by studying history and archeology of non-Western cultures and religions.

§

It wasn't so much that my views of the Bible changed, but rather that a few small seeds of doubt grew over the years. I became very interested in Astronomy at about age 14 (now my career), and my growing love of science helped the seeds of doubt grow. Also, through my early college years, it was becoming increasingly clear that I was gay (I was aware of this much earlier, but always found a way to deny it to myself, and try to "pray it away"). Ultimately it was my acceptance of my sexuality that pushed me out of the church and led to my de-conversion. This change occurred fairly suddenly, and was only difficult for a short time. It was only years later, in my late 20's and early 30's when I began coming out to friends as a gay man. They were all fine with it. My coming out experience to my parents in my mid 30's did not go well, and continues to not go well.

§

I entered a scriptural argument with another member of the group when we began comparing editions of the NIV. This prompted me to begin looking at the older versions and the word changes there. When I realized how much the Bible had changed over its years in English alone, and how much it had been filtered by its translation, I began to question how it could be the inerrant Word of God. No one in my faith could explain to me how these different variants of the "infallible" Bible with different interpretations squared with the notion that God could possibly intend for each of them to be the literal Word. It took me about 3 months to formalize this line of thinking, at which time I realized I was seeking my answers in the wrong places. I continued to maintain interest in the Bible, but only as a record of the progress of human thought.

§

I noticed inconsistencies that when I asked about them, we're waved aside. That bothered me. But what bothered me the most was the bible's words on the role of women and the evilness of homosexuality. I could not understand why god would care about what gender someone was, or why all women had to be submissive because of Eve.

§

I originally bought into the idea of the Bible as the infallible and inerrant Word of God, so I decided to read through the entire Bible and discovered several unsavory parts to it. I knew I would find accounts of human error, not excepting incest and rape, but reading sections that describe God as malicious and even deceptive started my doubts about the Bible.

§

I read the Bible, and decided its truthfulness was doubtful. Then, I read [Bertrand] Russell's "Why I Am Not a Christian," and realized that the Bible was nonsense.

§

After I began seminary school, I took a critical look at the Old Testament and New Testament and realized there were many outlandish claims concerning Jesus. I also learned the history of the Christian church and how the bible was put together. I discovered what a murderous religion Christianity was and I no longer wanted a part of it.

§

My views changed the more I read it. I had questions about what I read, and at first, I was able to rationalize the questions away. The more I read, the more questions I had, and then more I realized that if God is really as described by the Bible, I did not want to worship him. It was very hard at first, but became easier over time. It was probably about four years before I completely rejected the Bible as being a divine document of any nature.

§

My views changed only at the end, and fairly quickly, as I finally exposed myself to higher criticism. Perhaps unusually, I found the experience rather painless despite by previously intense faith.

§

Over several years of reading biblical criticisms rather than exclusively apologetic works.

§

I went from denomination to denomination as my interpretations changed. I thought the problem we with each group. Sola Scriptura has many problems, private interpretation being one of them. Once I was open to the possibility that the problem was the bible itself everything changed. I started reading Bart Ehrman and that was it. Once my eyes were opened to the truth they could not be closed again. It happened very quickly and with little difficulty for me. I love TRUTH more than anything. My commitment is to the truth

§

In my late 30s, I decided to investigate the historical figure of Jesus and the authenticity of the scriptures. I read considerably and was forced to conclude that the bible was a collection of entirely human documents. I was angry that I had not investigated this sooner and felt foolish at allowing myself to be misled. Sander's "Historical Figure of Jesus" dealt the fatal blow to my faith. It has taken me a year or so to reconstruct my moral boundaries based on my own opinions and readings.

§

My de-conversion took place over about two years. It started as I began to learn more about natural history and evolution. I began as a biblical literalist, and slowly, over about six months, my belief in the Genesis account was chipped away. After that I fairly quickly came to view the Bible as an errant but still divinely inspired document. The more I studied and thought about it, the less reliable any of it seemed. After another 6-8 months I firmly considered myself a deist and discounted the bible as nothing more than ancient writings. Within the next 10 months I had totally lost the ability to fool myself into believing in god any longer.

§

I was fighting against years of Christian-minded upbringing and that was the source of the challenge. It the challenge ended when I started looking at life through a wider lens, and everything was much clearer. From that point on, I viewed the Bible as more of a choke chain than a guiding hand. And this choke chain would have inhibited my growing into the person that I am today. I do not believe that the Bible is something to be taken literally, nor is it the infallible, only-game-in-town guide to life. To me it is, at best, a poorly-written work of fiction, and the interpretations of its readers have pitted much of humankind against one another and sucked humanity out of people.

§

I developed critical-thinking skills in my mid-twenties, having never been in a situation in which they were taught or even understood. From there, the gaping holes in the "history" claimed within the pages of the Bible became rather obvious.

§

I wrestled with doubts at many times. One of the first big issues was with a man I was dating. He told me I was not submissive enough. Apparently I needed to submit to anyone with a penis. I was very upset at God for making me a woman. Later, my skepticism was further stirred by a World Religions class. Everyone in the class made fun of people who believed other religions. How could they believe them, they asked? I thought Christianity seemed pretty unbelievable also.

§

In my teens, I began to notice inconsistencies in the Bible, and between Christian doctrine and what the text of the Bible actually says. Being naturally curious as I am, I started reading up on higher criticism and logically picking apart arguments in popular Christian apologetics. I took Greek in college, and took all of the (secular) classes I could on religion. I remained nominally Christian into my early 20s, albeit with softened views on the Bible/doctrine. Eventually, my intellectual integrity wouldn't let me keep up the charade. I ended up majoring in classical studies and anthropology, which has eventually led to my pursuing post-graduate study in near eastern languages and cultures. I find parts of the Bible quite interesting in a cultural/historical sense, while others are droll and hackneyed. I'm probably more well versed in it now, though, than 99% of "Bible believing" Christians!

§

I was grounded in the idea that every word of the Bible was truth, but as a teenager I began to have difficulty with the violence of the Old Testament and the problem of homosexuality. To excuse the OT, my mom convinced me that God was a just god and the violence was necessary. (I never really asked her about homosexuality.) While spending a year living alone in France (age 22) I decided to renew my relationship with Christ by reading through my entire Bible. This time, the Old Testament violence was absolutely too horrible to justify, and it kicked off the beginning of the end of my faith. As soon as I realized that parts of the Bible were probably untrue, I was unable to believe any of it.

§

While reading it from cover to cover, I began to discover that the character Yahweh and I had some pretty strong disagreements on morality. I didn't like his jealous, murderous nature and so the doubts were born. Then it hit me. "Talking snakes and donkeys?!? Every species of animal from every continent on a ship?!? For real?"

§

I came to realize that the stories and claims in the Bible were not consistent with my experience with the world around me, and that they were much more likely to be simply another mythological system. The process took place over a few months, with a long period beforehand in which I attempted to understand the Bible in a more metaphorical sense.

§

Since I was taught a literal interpretation of the Bible, I believed that it must contain no errors or contradictions whatsoever. If it did, then it was not perfect, and therefore could not be what it was claimed to be. Eventually I became more aware of glaring contradictions within the Bible, as well as inconsistencies between the claims and stories of the Bible and various "common sense" notions of reality and morality.

§

Contradictions within the Bible and with the observable world caused me to question what I was being taught; this went on for years. The very fact of having questions was very scary and was something I tried to suppress.

§

Oh goodness, that's quite the question. Near the end of high school I started waffling between the Bible being the 'infallible, inerrant Word of God' and 'Word of God, written by men under divine inspiration.' It always seemed unlikely to me that God spoke the Bible word for word and the various men just transcribed it. As I thought about it more, I came to the conclusion that men wrote the Bible, but God supervised. There wasn't anything in the Bible that he didn't specifically want there. As I went through college, I had a boyfriend who was into religious studies courses. He had taken them for a better understanding of the Bible, but soon found himself kind of shaken out of his firm belief. I am a big history fan, and as I started to learn more about early Jewish history, I started to doubt the Bible more. If I'm going to believe something, I want it to be historically accurate. I had many discussions bordering on arguments with my boyfriend, but over the course of college my view changed to 'significant cultural document.' Since deconverting, I've read a lot more and thought more critically about the Bible and have downgraded it further. I believe it's interesting to examine as a cultural document, but shouldn't be afforded any extra special place over other documents of antiquity.

§

Read [Bart Ehrman's] *Misquoting Jesus*, it opened my eyes.

§

After no longer being brainwashed into believing the infallibility of the Bible, I further realized it also has so truly abhorrent things in it that Christians somehow must justify in order to believe in their religion. Horrible genocides, infanticide, rape, incest...but somehow you have to accept it as "good" because God sanctioned it despite the obvious realization that it really is filled with horror. To say those things are wrong would be challenging God and no Christian ever does that. He would punish you and you'd be ostracized from your support and community group. Given how nice Christians often are, I can see why many people don't ever question it.

§

I began reading the works of Christopher Hitchens and Richard Dawkins, and unfortunately, I admit, Ayn Rand, which turned me into a much more rational thinker, at least philosophically. I had doubt, but I still hadn't come to terms with my far right-wing positions on social issues. I happened to be a closeted gay man throughout my teens, so as I came to terms with my sexuality, I eventually turned my liberal on social issues. When the voters in my home state of Maine voted down our marriage equality law, I started to further re-think my alliance with those on the far-right. It was after that shock, that I started to realize the world wasn't so scary without God, that in fact, it was quite the reverse. People who believed in God made my state a worse of place for gay people and their families. Reading and listening to Hitchens, James Randi, Penn & Teller and co. helped in the conversion as well. By my early twenties, I was comfortable to call myself an agnostic my default, maybe even a very liberal theist. I now fully embrace the term atheist to describe myself, and while like most other humans, I fear my death, I'm no longer concerned about being condemned to damnation for eternity. And I'm certainly not expecting some old man a robe to be greeting me in the clouds.

§

Losing my faith was miserable and horrific and lonely and painful. But, I had studied a good deal of history of the Bible and Judaism and felt I had no choice but to no longer believe I had been told the truth growing up. I alienated myself from Conservative Christianity at 17 after reading "Les Miserables" and I called myself an atheist at 20.

§

I took an "Intro to the New Testament" religion class at FSU, and learned about how the claims of biblical authorship made by pastors and apologists were completely unfounded. After that, it was an education in science that began to peel one layer of fundamentalism after another away until I began to see the bible as a human work of ancient, ignorant racists and misogynists. To be honest, while I don't think that the bible is any more special than any other book, I would go farther and say that it's one of the most socially-damaging books that the human race has ever produced, along with Mein Kampf and Mao's Red Book.

§

I started to question the quite obvious contradictions...I decided to piece together for myself a "correct" Easter story, using only the Gospels, and I couldn't pinpoint an exact day of the week of the "Last Supper." I asked around to friends, other bible study leaders, even a pastor, and no one could really give me a good answer. After that I started just being more skeptical about the bible, and about what it said--especially when it came to the roles and place of women. It was very slow, just random little thoughts here and there, and I kept my thoughts to myself for the most part--I was a bible study leader myself, and couldn't let people know I was having these doubts about the bible. Most of the time whenever I had a doubt, I brought myself back with the "it's not for me to know" reason. I do know that I started to question when and how the bible was put together, and as I was de-converting (my deconversion process was less about biblical text than how Christians treated me and social issues), that became THE reason I finally left. I couldn't see how a religion based on an incorrect and fallible text could be true.

§

In an effort to become a better Xian, to hone my skills as a preacher, I started reading the bible with a zeal. I wanted to know it all. It took 3 years, a gradual process with much thought. When it hit me, that it was all bullshit, I was mad, sad and scared. I hadn't yet learned about evolution, about life, although I was 38, I was scared. I started reaching out on blogs, I started talking online to other freethinkers. Slowly but surely I came to a happy understanding. It was probably the most depressing thing I've ever endured. Now I see it as rather silly.

§

Once I started really reading the Bible, my faith started to wane heavily. Too many contradictions, too many unbelievable things. The more it was pressed as God's truth, the more I questioned it.

§

My de-conversion commenced over a period of maybe a year or two. I started questioning

§

I read the bible and was deeply hurt by the rampant violence and sexism. I eventually discovered through Catholic friends that not everyone thinks the Bible is the complete, infallible word of god.

§

The more I studied the Bible, the more I doubted. A tipping point occurred when I began a Bible study group at my public high school, and learned first hand that other protestant denominations interpreted some scriptures in other ways than my church. I could no longer believe that MY Southern Baptist church was the one true church with the one true beliefs. After that realization I began to question the authority of my parents and church leaders. Later on I began to learn about Catholicism and Christian history, at which point the whole belief system unraveled.

§

I learned more about the history of the events purported to have taken place in the Bible and began to see the book as a guide to live by more than the inspired word of God. Then, I went through a very difficult time during which I prayed and prayed, focusing on the scripture that indicates that if you believe totally that God will grant you what you pray for. Let's just say that that is not what happened. Some other events culminated in my questioning further during that time -- a time when I was very faithful and obedient. Then I started reading Hitchens and Dawkins.

§

It started in a bible class on the synoptic gospels where contradictions were pointed out, to a study of the Skeptic's Annotated Bible to firm up my faith were I realized the flood story was very specific and impossible, to an acceptance of evolution and the realization that the whole Adam/fall into sin story is just impossible. Since Adam's fall is critical to Paul's theology, and in general without a fall from perfection into sin theodicies don't make sense, the salvation story is bunk, etc, this was the beginning of the end of Christianity for me.

§

The book of Job is what really got me thinking. In it, God appears to be a vain rube, easily duped by Satan. Under Satan's influence, the perfect god's creation gets him to throw his most devout follower under the bus, just to prove a point. Ridiculous.

§

I recall a sermon in which the lead pastor of my church referred to a scripture having to do with getting tattoos and how it was against the word of God. I recall him saying specifically "Do you believe the bible is correct and is the infallible instruction of God or not? There is no middle ground". It struck me as so strange, because his son was in the midst of an adultery scandal and I knew the bible had some pretty harsh judgments for people who cheated. For whatever reason, that was the first time I finally realized that he was actually right, the bible either is, or is not the infallible word of God. After reading a bit more I realized that there were so many fairy tales and inaccuracies in the bible and that there is no way they could be the product of some all knowing god. I think it all came crashing down after I really started to dissect the bible from an intellectually honest standpoint. There was no force of will that could keep me believing in something so obviously made up.

§

I read the entire Bible, and the inconsistencies, errors, and obvious human origin caused me to re-evaluate my faith

§

The more I studied, the more obvious these problems were and the more clear it became that the reason no one was offering me a solution was because there WERE no solutions. I was taught that the bible was 100% perfect fact, and as soon as I realized that could not possibly be true the rest of it sort of fell apart.

§

A friend gave me a "test" about things that happened in the bible. Unbeknownst to me, the answer to all questions was "all of the above." It was designed to point out biblical contradictions by showing the bible says completely different things about the same event. That started the process. It took another 10 years probably before I simply dismissed the bible as mostly fictional.

§

The obvious flaws in the Bible helped lead to my loss of faith. I remember thinking that with all the competing religious texts that if one were actually the Word of God, it would be stand above the others in some clear way, which the Bible did not seem to do.

§

The impetus was discovering / learning / researching the origins of the canon, authorship, authenticity, etc. It took around 18 months for all of this to sink in. Today I believe as I indicated above, that it is a cultural document, but nothing more special than any other religious text.

Question 15: If an encounter with "higher criticism" and/or liberal (non-fundamentalist) interpretations of the Bible were contributing factors in the process of rejecting Christian faith and adopting agnosticism/atheism, how important a role did this play?

Formerly →	All Respondents Except CEF Christians N=1170	Easter-Christmas Christian, with Some Sunday Schooling N=468	Devout Liberal-Moderate Catholic N=262	Devout Conservative Catholic N=75	Devout Liberal-Moderate Protestant N=365	Devout CEF Protestant N=391
Very important	21.3%	18.6%	20.2%	25.3%	24.7%	28.3%
Somewhat important	30.1%	27.4%	32.8%	16.0%	34.5%	26.1%
Not that important	15.3%	15.4%	16.8%	9.3%	15.3%	14.8%
Not part of the process	33.3%	38.7%	30.6%	49.3%	25.5%	30.7%

Question 16: When you were Christian (before the deconversion process commenced), what did you believe about origins?

Formerly →	All Respondents Except CEF Christians N=1170	Easter-Christmas Christian, with Some Sunday Schooling N=468	Devout Liberal-Moderate Catholic N=262	Devout Conservative Catholic N=75	Devout Liberal-Moderate Protestant N=365	Devout CEF Protestant N=391
Everything was created by God exactly as the book of Genesis records	15.0%	14.7%	8.0%	30.7%	17.0%	59.8%
Everything was created by God, but Genesis is a metaphor for God's creative work	31.4%	28.6%	31.3%	28.0%	35.6%	25.3%
Everything was created by God specifically through the agency of evolution (e.g. Francis Collins' view)	37.4%	31.6%	47.7%	36.0%	37.5%	13.8%
Life on Earth came to be by natural means	16.3%	25.0%	13.0%	5.3%	9.9%	1.0%

Question 17: How would you describe your views about origins now?						
Formerly →	All Respondents Except CEF Christians N=1170	Easter-Christmas Christian, with Some Sunday Schooling N=468	Devout Liberal-Moderate Catholic N=262	Devout Conservative Catholic N=75	Devout Liberal-Moderate Protestant N=365	Devout CEF Protestant N=391
Everything was created by God exactly as the book of Genesis records	0.1%	0.0%	0.0%	1.3%	0.0%	0.8%
Everything was created by God, but Genesis is a metaphor for God's creative work	0.3%	0.0%	0.8%	0.0%	0.3%	0.8%
Everything was created by God specifically through the agency of evolution (e.g. Francis Collins' view)	1.8%	1.3%	1.9%	2.7%	2.2%	2.3%
Life on Earth came to be by natural means	97.9%	98.7%	97.3%	96.0%	97.5%	96.2%

Question 18: If your views of origins changed during your years as a Christian and leading up to your de-conversion, what was the impetus for that change, how difficult was that change, over how long a period did the change occur, and what did you end up believing about origins? Please use as much space as you wish.

Selected Responses[52] of Respondents Identifying as Formerly Conservative / Evangelical / Fundamentalist Protestant (298 of 391 submitted a written response):

As my deconversion progressed, I adopted the stance that God supernaturally eliminated evidence of a 6000 year old creation as a test of our faith. Once I deconverted, I concluded that the Christian god never created the world/universe.

§

The second I undertook the scientific method there was no room left for faith in things without evidence. Evolution changed everything for me. It's so beautiful to see the mechanism which creates such wonderful things without the need for magic of any kind. So much more elegant, and completely within the realm of human understanding.

§

There are two versions of the creation of earth in Genesis. If God wrote the bible wouldn't he know how he created the earth?

§

Evolution made so much sense to me, even as a kid. The natural explanations for our existence was so damned hard to deny, but I managed to until my deconversion process. I can remember praying to god to take my life before I could be

---

[52] Represented here are eleven of sixty (11 of 60) pages submitted in the FCNA Survey. Submissions in **bold** were cited, in whole or in part, in the text of the paper. Printed here as submitted.

convinced that the natural explanations were true. I knew suicide wasn't an option. (In the Church of Christ, one can bet on a trip to hell if one commits suicide). Even if suicide were a viable option according to what I believed, I don't know that I would have gone through with it, but I would have believed death preferable to the damnation that would result from loosing my faith.

§

I lost my faith in the Bible before I accepted the possibility that evolution was true. Then I studied evolution and took classes in anthropology and realized that it's a science that is well supported by evidence, facts, and even math.

§

Learning about evolution…did play a large role in my deconversion. The evidence for evolution is immense and is consistent with it being a natural and unguided force.

§

Accepting evolution as true was the first nail in the Christianity coffin.

§

Creationism was the root, I figured, of everything wrong with the church; the fear of knowledge and the sheltering of your own to protect them from facts. If facts were so dangerous, I wondered, was the religion so fragile that it could be destroyed by more knowledge? For me, the answer was yes, and it was a good thing to learn the truth, even if it wasn't the truth I wanted.

§

I slowly came to the conclusion that it was more likely for the universe to have started as an energy collision, not from divine intervention.

§

The Bible generally became irrelevant in relation to origins; or no more relevant than other creation myths.

I was always a science girl. Evolution was always the answer for me, so it wasn't a tough leap to go from god started it to the big bang once I was out of the church. But later becoming a full on atheist, science had a tremendous role in my rejection of the god hypothesis.

§

I used to believe, when I was very young, that God created the world just as the Bible described in Genesis. As I got older, into my teens, I began to believe that the creation story of Genesis was more of a metaphor and that God still created it, and I accepted that God might have created the process of evolution because I couldn't ignore the scientific evidence for evolution. I decided that I was no longer a Christian at around age 19, and now I believe that the origin of the world was a completely natural occurrence. I came to these conclusions because of what we know about the world thanks to science, and because I find the idea that some sort of god had to create us in order for us to exist preposterous. I'm going to stick with science, since it can actually credibly provide evidence for things.

§

As I studied science (particularly biomolecular chemistry as it relates to the human central nervous system), I began to slowly reject my view of religious origin of life on earth. This rejection slowly spread to a rejection of religion entirely as a means of adequately explaining or theorizing about the origins of the earth, life, and the universe.

§

I could no longer defend the Bible and ignore all of the scientific evidence.

§

I probably let go of the idea of divine origin pretty early in the process. My limited education about evolution was sufficient to convince me that another mechanism was far more likely.

§

Education in school about evolution helped me to begin the process, although I initially resisted it, as my doubts about the religion developed it became important that I knew about the theory of evolution as an alternate explanation for life. Again, it was a gradual and progressive change over a period of several years. And, with time it has only become easier to see the world in natural terms as years go by.

§

I accepted science once I learned it. Science always made sense to me in a way that religion never did. Religion was a matter of rigging my Biblical interpretation to match the science. But eventually that became too difficult.

§

I was always interested in science. Over time, the two (science/religion) merged. As I learned more of science, the religious belief would be adjusted to accommodate those facts and accepted theories.

§

I discovered that the anti-evolution books sold by my church were full of deliberate lies and omissions about Darwin and the theory of evolution. I have never believed that lying should ever play a role in educating people on a topic.

§

Once I started to question the wisdom of the Bible, it snowballed very quickly from doubt to outright disbelief. **It was very difficult, because my entire youth had been founded in the absolute perfection of the Word of God, and I wanted so much to believe.** However, once faith evaporated, the Bible didn't hold up to scrutiny. Science did hold up to scrutiny.

§

The process began in college, where I took many biology and zoology courses. I came to learn what evolution really was (as opposed to the fundy straw man version) and became familiar with the mountains of evidence supporting the theory. It was all downhill from that point. The entire process took about 3 years, all told.

§

After rejecting religion, the study habits I had invested in scriptures turned to books on science and skepticism.

§

I was taught evolution was wrong, silly and evil until I was a teenager and my mom became fascinated by Charles Darwin. I eventually took biology in college and learned more about it but I still don't know very much about Evolution. I don't believe in Creation as taught in the Bible at all, though. It's just a silly myth like any other creation myth.

§

With the cognitive dissonance of religion gone, I was free to embrace a logical approach to knowledge.

§

As a child, I took Genesis (and all the Bible) literally. As a teen (converted) I began wondering about the time frames of Genesis and vaguely saw that those weren't feasible with even the most BASIC science of a universe some 10-15 billion years old. During either late senior high and/or college, I began finding inconsistencies and outright falsehoods in what I'd begun learning as "Christian Evidences," specifically the issues that are now called "Intelligent Design."

§

Mostly through education in general -- history, biology, geology -- all played a role. The de-conversion began as early as when I was about 14 but didn't come into completion until my fifth year of college, when I was 23.

§

I began undoing everything I had come to believe in like shedding a garment made of spider webs. I went to college and studied psychology and biology. This was very helpful in recovery.

§

I took my first biology class....end of story.

§

When I went away to college, I got a real science education for the first time. I had steeled myself in preparation for my "faith coming under attack" but instead was shocked to learn that evolution made sense.

§

I was always skeptical of Genesis, as long as I can remember. The church told us one thing, but my parents (especially my mother in private) would admit that maybe there was some room for interpretation. When I became very serious about science and studied physics in college, I became comfortable with just NOT KNOWING. I think that's one thing that fundamentalists cannot say--they must know the answer. "The answer is in the Bible." But I have become more comfortable, as a scientist, in just not knowing. It's okay to not know. But science is the best tool we have to get to the truth.

§

The impetus for change was the internet, in specific the science podcasting universe. I first listened because science is cool, and began to actual think about what I believed. My belief system was a house of cards, and once the first one fell they all came crashing down. My first defense against evolution was to be ignorant of what it was actually saying. Next line of defense was to point out that regardless of evolution, Jesus still died for me, so debating about the origins was silly and pointless. However, as I began to critically examine what I believed in, I decided evolution by natural selection made the most sense, provided the best evidence, and presented a logical argument for reality.

§

Just got tired of all the intellectual "overhead" and mental gymnastic required to sustain/defend a creationist system. The honesty or piety my religious beliefs nurtured in me required that I could no longer defend such tripe.

§

I suppose it was a long time in the making but once I understood the natural view of life my previous religious views of origins were gone. All it took was the first couple chapters of Dawkins book "The Greatest Show on Earth"--at the start of the book I was creationist and by the end I was excited that I had at last discovered the wonders of evolution. I now believe in a natural world and natural origins with no god what so ever.

§

I took an Anthropology course where I learned a great deal, and it was during that course that I became convinced that evolution was true and then all of my beliefs in the bible and god came crashing down like a house of cards.

§

I took courses in astronomy which convinced me evolution was true. I also took classes in paleontology which convinced me evolution was true and I also listened to testimony in court against Intelligent Design which also convinced me evolution was true. I accept evolution as truth because it does not involve magic and invisible super friends to create life.

§

Science education ranging from geology to biology led me to question the biblical story. This developed over the course of teenage years to outright rejection of the biblical creation story.

§

In fact, the creation story is what prompted me to critically analyze the rest of the bible, and to start seeing the logical inconsistencies.

§

I encountered information about biology, evolution, cosmology, theoretical physics, philosophy that all became the impetus for change in my faith.

§

I was a Young Earther for years. Once I realized the story of Genesis was myth, I accepted evolution. Francis Collins' actually convinced me of evolution by reading his book. I don't think that was his intention. God is completely unnecessary

§

I always loved science as a kid, and excelled in math and sciences before getting roped in by the youth group. I managed to come up with some compelling rationalizations on my own back then that now smell like Intelligent Design. To take a supernatural being out of the equation was simple. The same processes at work, now just no hand behind any of it.

§

Education is the death of fundamentalism in my opinion. I would now consider myself to be a naturalist. I completely reject the notion of the supernatural.

§

I was taught by my mother that the world was less than 6000 years old and that evolution was a myth created by the devil. But in school, as I learned about physical science, I loved what I was hearing and loved that it could be tested and proven, so I developed my own ideas of intelligent design to allow for science and myth to coexist in my mind.

§

It was my study of biology and especially of evolution that caused me to doubt and finally leave the faith. Despite joining CRS, ICR and attending debates, writing letters, I found the creationists poorly knowledgeable and would later find that the early creationists got many of their "advanced degrees" from diploma mills. The deceit really stung and I never could forgive a Christian for lying for Christ or equally bad being incompetent. I felt betrayed. It was difficult leaving - the close relationships, shared prayers, the warm and welcoming community and many years later it would cost me my 37 yr. old marriage as our world views collided and exploded into pieces of regret for our children. I could no longer remain silent as my then wife told our children lies about origins, the basis of every world view.

§

I adamantly rejected/mocked the idea of evolution. I avoided science classes because I did not want to be confronted or have to confront evolution any more than necessary. During my 12-18 month deconversion process, I began to allow myself to consider the details of evolution and found it a very compelling and fascinating idea. Once the Bible wasn't true, it was not too hard to understand the ideas that had previously seemed ridiculous and impossible.

§

I took science and history classes in college that made me realize origin myths exist in all cultures, and they fade over time. Why not this one as well?

§

Thank you Dawkins. The anti-evolution message was forced from an early age, but his books helped clarify the facts.

§

I did not really consider origins until the later phases of my deconversion process. The impetus for that change was conversations with scientifically minded friends, and reading secular books. At the end, I actively sought out popular science books on evolution (The Selfish Gene, The Extended Phenotype, various books by Sagan, etc) in an attempt to compensate for my utterly misguided Christian high school education.

§

The information that I'd been taught by my church about evolution was so wrong. Accepting and understanding evolution was a very difficult process for me. It took until my final year of college, and another evolution class, for me to really feel like I had a grasp on it. We may not know the exact origin of the universe, but I feel like evolution offers the explanation for how our planet came to be the way it is.

§

My deconversion was all about origins. At one time I believed all the various positions (young earth, old earth, etc.), with evolution as the final one.

§

I became an evolutionist about 2 years ago, after finally accepting the majority scientific view, and it was really a world-changing perspective for me as a Baptist fundamentalist.

§

Once I started looking at the bible as a book similar to Grimm's Fairy Tales or Aesop's Fables, it became clear that scientists did a better job of backing up their beliefs than creationists did with theirs.

§

After my EvilBible.com experience, I made the assumption that scientific claims on the origin of life were true. It was not until I took Biology and Geology courses as an undergrad that these theories unraveled themselves before me. After learning basic biology and geology, my Atheism was strengthened.

§

Prior to college I thought that evolution was a faulty and unreliable hypothesis of scientists. Taking science classes in college cured me of that misconception.

§

De-conversion was a moderately long process - 40 years in I'm still not sure it is over. Ultimately, reality was the impetus for the change. One can only deny observed facts for so long. The logical rules of evolution are elegant. The mountain of evidence for evolution just never ends. Denying it is pointless.

§

Learning about the science of evolution is what pushed me over the edge on and began my de-conversion.

§

My belief was based on an understanding that the Bible was completely true. As that belief clashed with actual facts and evidence, it became clear that the truth wasn't not found in the Bible, but in science.

Question 19: If an understanding of evolution and naturalism as a satisfactory explanation of origins and life on earth were contributing factors in the process of rejecting Christian faith and adopting agnosticism / atheism, how important a role did this play?

Formerly →	All Respondents Except CEF Christians N=1170	Easter-Christmas Christian, with Some Sunday Schooling N=468	Devout Liberal-Moderate Catholic N=262	Devout Conservative Catholic N=75	Devout Liberal-Moderate Protestant N=365	Devout CEF Protestant N=391
Very important	36.7%	39.3%	37.0%	25.3%	35.3%	42.2%
Somewhat important	26.6%	27.6%	23.7%	26.7%	27.4%	25.3%
Not that important	15.9%	14.5%	15.6%	12.0%	18.6%	13.8%
Not part of the process	20.9%	18.6%	23.7%	36.0%	18.6%	18.7%

Question 20: When you were Christian (before the deconversion process commenced), how did you view science?						
Formerly →	All Respondents Except CEF Christians N=1170	Easter-Christmas Christian, with Some Sunday Schooling N=468	Devout Liberal-Moderate Catholic N=262	Devout Conservative Catholic N=75	Devout Liberal-Moderate Protestant N=365	Devout CEF Protestant N=391
Science had its place and should not overstep that place	4.9%	4.5%	4.6%	13.3%	3.8%	9.7%
Science had its place but religious / Bible truth trumped scientific truth when they seemed to contradict each other	11.2%	7.3%	9.9%	17.3%	15.9%	51.2%
Science and religion were both means of understand the world, from different perspectives (e.g., Stephen J. Gould's idea about "non-overlapping magisterial)	57.2%	51.5%	63.4%	52.0%	61.1%	32.2%
Science was the best means of understand-ing life and alleviating suffering	26.8%	36.8%	22.1%	17.3%	19.2%	6.9%

Question 21: How would you describe your views of science now?						
Formerly →	All Respondents Except CEF Christians N=1170	Easter-Christmas Christian, with Some Sunday Schooling N=468	Devout Liberal-Moderate Catholic N=262	Devout Conservative Catholic N=75	Devout Liberal-Moderate Protestant N=365	Devout CEF Protestant N=391
Science had its place and should not overstep that place	0.6%	0.4%	0.8%	2.7%	0.3%	0.5%
Science had its place but religious / Bible truth trumped scientific truth when they seemed to contradict each other	0.2%	0.0%	0.0%	1.3%	0.3%	0.3%
Science and religion were both means of understand the world, from different perspectives (e.g., Stephen J. Gould's idea about "non-overlapping magisterial)	9.0%	8.1%	9.5%	5.3%	10.4%	6.1%
Science was the best means of understand-ing life and alleviating suffering	90.3%	91.5%	89.7%	90.7%	89.0%	93.1%

Question 22: If your views of science changed during your years as a Christian and leading up to your de-conversion, what was the impetus for that change, how difficult was that change, over how long a period did that change occur, and what did you end up believing about science? Please use as much space as you wish.

Selected Responses[53] of Respondents Identifying as Formerly Conservative / Evangelical / Fundamentalist Protestant (255 of 391 submitted a written response):

I have always loved science, I just figured they were making some claims out of a rejection of god rather than based on the facts. But the more and more I learned the more I realized they actually knew what the heck they were talking about.

§

I believe that the scientific method is the only way we can objectively know anything.

§

I always respected science and seemed compartmentalized from religion until I began to pose questions of my own.

§

Once I started doing research on the origins of the Old and New Testament, reading scientific articles and books by authors like Stephen Hawkings, Brian Greene and others, it was as if a deep hunger was finally being satisfied. This wonderful journey took me about ten years.

§

I see it as more credible now and how poorly misunderstood many scientific concepts have been. I realize that Christians have "demonized" science and science has fought back...

---

[53] Represented here are twelve of forty-three (12 of 43) pages submitted in the FCNA Survey. Submissions in **bold** were cited, in whole or in part, in the text of the paper. Printed here as submitted.

I always enjoyed playing with bugs when I was a kid and loved all things science. I had to keep "two minds" about it--one for church and one for what I was seeing. I had to grow up and get away from the family before I realized I needed only one mind.

§

I'm a biology and neuroscience double major. In learning the more in-depth rigors of the study, it was impossible for me to view science as anything less than the best hope humanity has for a rational, fair society and an understanding of the world.

§

The more I read outside of the Christian bubble, the more exposed I became to scientific thought that wasn't filtered through an agenda.

§

I believed we should be consistent. We can't accept the scientific method when it prevents or treats diseases, makes our cars run better or feeds millions of people and turn around and reject it when its conclusions diverge from our most cherished religious beliefs.

§

I had been told and choose to believe that non-Christian scientists had formed a conspiracy because they like to sin against God. Eventually I realized it's silly to mischaracterize like that. Scientists are just following the evidence they find in a search for truth.

§

I used to believe that science was a search for truth. It facilitated religion, but when it contradicted it, faith always trumped logical conjecture. I believed that religion was the inherent truth; that humans only needed to utilize science as a means of understanding that truth. As I ventured into university-level science, I began to view both religion and science in a different light. Religion became an archaic way of understanding the world and dealing with unexplained or uncopeable social/political/economical/natural phenomena. Science became man's search for a means of explaining and extricating what he believed to be the truth of the natural world. Thus, instead of science being a search for truth, it is simply a "best guess" or "best fit" ideology of how the natural world functions the way it does and how mankind may best use that knowledge (whether it truly be the base operating mechanism of that particular system or not).

§

My views about science changed rather quickly in line with my views of origins and had a direct effect on my deconversion.

§

Science was not as important to me before, b/c I didn't think I or anyone really needed it, since one's relationship with God was all that really mattered, and true/worthwhile knowledge was supposed to come from God and scripture. When the accuracy of the Bible turned out to be absurd, I was pleased to discover just how fun and amazing science really was, and how much work had gone into discovery, and how much people really had discovered about evolution and various other aspects of science. I now subscribe to sciencedaily.com to keep abreast of new discoveries in neuroscience, evolution, etc. Science became a source of entertainment, inspiration, amazement, wonder, respect, and ever-increasing knowledge.

§

My view of science has only changed in that I don't view it as an abstract monster that wants to eat God anymore.

§

Once I had philosophically reasoned that the Christian god was false, I felt compelled to accept a naturalistic model. Therefore, I read a lot of books, took several science courses in college, and participated in public science conferences. This was the last part of a deconversion process, so about the last year of a 4 year total process. This was the least difficult part of the deconversion.

§

Not that interested in science before de-conversion, now I can't get enough.

§

I was skeptical of science as a Christian because I felt it was infringing on the ultimate truth of god. Now I am skeptical of pretty much everything but science. This view shifted as I took psychology courses in college and began to see the ignorance of most everyone in forming beliefs (myself included). When my own aunt tried to convince me that aliens built the pyramids I thought it was time to become more educated in science to combat the rise of pseudoscience and supernaturalism. Michael Shermer, Carl Sagan and James Randi as well as the Skepticality, Monstertalk and Point of Inquiry podcasts have been very helpful in this area.

§

I understand evolution and genetic information now. I had refused this in the past.

§

Learning who can be trusted is a powerful impetus. We had been brainwashed into distrusting everyone but our ministers. Even when they did get caught in sordid affairs excuses were made for them, "Satan has tempted them..." I had to learn to trust my own mind and believe that science is a noble profession rather than a tool of the devil. The first two years were the most crucial. After that I began to suspect that the outcome of my questions would always lead me away from Christian indoctrination. I ended up seeing science as a collection of great thinkers who had their own resistance to superstition in pursuit of reason.

§

I developed a greater understanding and appreciation for statistical reasoning and the aims and nature of scientific inquiry, and as this occurred, I grew less and less interested in religious groups and their activity. My interest in "science" didn't "push out" or nullify my religious education or experience, per se. I was already disgusted by the convenient moralisms, bumpersticker mentalisms and intellectual inconsistencies that were preached and perpetuated by the religious right I had known since infancy.

§

From my high school years until I officially resigned from my church at the age of 30 science played an ever increasing role in my life. As I recognized that certain of my beliefs were demonstrably untrue, those beliefs made way for new understanding. Basically I reached a point where there was so little of my faith left to cling to I simply quit trying. It wasn't a sudden change, but a gradual shift over time.

§

The scientific method is our best tool for discovering truth about our universe.

§

I started to doubt in college during my neuroscience and psychology courses. I didn't want to explore it further but was introduced to several podcasts and websites that I began listening to/reading and could no longer ignore the fact that I was losing my faith.

§

The extreme creationist claims to which I was exposed were simply self-discrediting, i.e., it simply claimed too much and appeared to me to be increasingly ludicrous and self-defeating. I gradually withdraw my investment in it; it's more the case that I gradually refused to defend it than anything else.

§

My views of science changed once I rejected my Christian beliefs, not before.

§

Science always fascinated. As belief faded, science simply came to seem more central.

§

I had always been interested in science, but I don't think that my interest in science was part of the impetus for leaving religion. By the time I was in college, my appreciation for science was much higher. Now, science is a huge part of my identity. Watching Carl Sagan's Cosmos is like a religious experience for me. I watch it beginning to end at least a few times a year. My love of science may have pushed me from agnosticism to atheism, but I'm not sure.

§

I read Robert Ingersoll's "Why I Am an Agnostic". Beautiful. Then I read others of like mind, and continued doing so and a whole new world of people opened up to me. Had I been introduced to these freethinkers earlier in my life, I'm sure I would have been in their troops and my own life would have been so much more enriched and beautiful. (Sigh)

§

Science was the major factor in my movement away from Christianity. Without science, I would probably still be preaching.

§

Cosmology had the most influence in my de-conversion and it became the foundation for my scientific views. The change was difficult, extremely mentally painful, and I face persecution and rejection on many sides socially. This process was about 5 years long.

§

As I studied anthropology and history and saw how the human view of the universe had changed over time, I slowly began to embrace science more and religion less. It was a slow change throughout my religious life.

§

My view of science as the most reliable foundation on which to place any perspective, has mostly developed after de-conversion, after my former foundation of faith in God vanished from below my feet.

§

The impetus for change was my love for learning from nature based tv shows and reading. The wool was pulled away from my eyes when the tv was turned on to PBS.

§

As a Christian, I had a fundamental misunderstanding of science and I deeply mistrusted scientists. I was told that we can be sure that Genesis is correct, and therefore any supposed evidence of evolution is either misunderstanding or misrepresentation of data on the part of the scientific community. Once I no longer believed that evolution was false, I was able to really understand the scientific method and what that concept means for science as a field of study.

§

My views of Science changed quite a lot. The impetus for change was simply not being able to turn a blind eye to what I came to view as superior explanations. This change came fairly easily even though the actual faith issues were a very hard change for me. This change came very quickly after I jettisoned my faith. I now see Science as the best methodology we currently have for investigating the natural world and seeking human progress.

§

I had absolutely no interest in science until after I deconverted, and even then only after a friend practically forced me to read Carl Sagan's "The Demon Haunted World: Science as a Candle in the Dark." I think that book, more than any other, has made me a naturalist rather than simply an atheist.

§

Really my views of science changed as my views of philosophy changed. Primarily I began to trust more and more in reason and less on intuition, and with this came an obvious increase in my awareness of the importance of science.

§

It was not until the final stage of my deconversion from agnosticism into atheism that I accepted science as the best and most logical means for explaining the universe.

§

I think the hypocrisy of Christians rejecting science when they disagree with it (evolution) yet all too eager to obtain life-saving science for their premature (19th) babies is one of the factors changing my views about science.

§

I began to see significant disagreements between the Bible's concept of how the human mind works, as well as the Bible's claims regarding the causes of mental illnesses and "sin." It was at this point, more than any other, that I truly felt that I had to choose between a scientific view and a religious one. I wanted to choose a religious views, but I couldn't ignore truths that I had experienced firsthand, and this was all in addition to the other plentiful difficulties I had with religion by that point. Ultimately, I came to trust science over religion, which implied that I could not use any religious document as a guide to reality, which left me with no alternative but a secular view.

§

It didn't take long and it wasn't hard to switch over to believing in science when I was told that I should stop taking my allergy and asthma medication because those ailments were a trick to test my faithfulness and they were all in my head and God would heal me of them if I were a

better believer. Then I wound up in the hospital with an oxygen count of 32% because I was having an asthma attack for three days straight and just trying to pray harder. I do have to say that I think I didn't die from the attack because I remained calm the entire time since I was praying and taking long, deep breaths instead of panicking and hyper-ventilating like I think I would have if I wasn't trying to pray harder. I was lucky enough to go to school on Monday morning and a teacher took me to the ER. I learned a valuable lesson that when I have an asthma attack to calm myself down and breath as deep as I can and hold it so that I am getting all the oxygen I can until I can get to my inhaler. Praying doesn't do a single thing, but medication sure does!

§

The advancement of science does leave for a more and more unemployed God

§

Science was a major factor in my change from believer to skeptic.

§

Basically I learned more science, and it destroyed my Christian faith/theology.

§

I now find science as the best method for knowledge and to "make the world a better place."

§

My views of science were always repressed, every time I learned something I was told that it was wrong. I loved science growing up and eventually learned to keep my scientific beliefs a secret because at that time it was hard for me to defend them. My views didn't REALLY change that much I just had to fight myself inside on what I

learned from teachers and what my Grandparents would say.

§

I began to see science as increasingly more useful, to the point that I am now convinced that science (and mathematics) is humanity's only useful tool for uncovering the unknown aspects of reality. "Divine revelation" just can't hold up to scrutiny.

§

I never gave science much credibility beyond the practical inventions, until I began researching origins and learning a little bit of biology and genetics. I feel as if I have ignored an ocean of truth to concentrate on a puddle of "religious knowledge" that I called my world. This too was very difficult, not for me personally to accept, but to get others (fundamentalists) to accept on my behalf. I failed. Now I simply do not talk about it to these people, but I no longer respect them as I once did, because they were willfully ignorant. My feelings on this are tempered by the fact that I too was willingly ignorant for a long time.

§

I firmly believe that science is how one connects to the natural world. If one truly wants to get in touch with the universe as we know it, the best of all possible ways is to study it. I've always liked sciences, but was scared of mathematics. As a returning student, I'm trying to study everything. Studying astronomy, biology, geology, physics on the astrological scale as well as the atomic.

§

My view of science has been the same since I was a small child. I always revered it as an awesome and magnificent achievement of man. I never really thought the two shared equal quests. Religion pursued the spiritual and science the natural. I guess I viewed science as a means to find God via the natural since it was near impossible to find physical evidence of the supernatural. I no longer view religion in the same respect and science is no longer tied into by any means.

§

I thought that science was an area of study like any other, subject to human error. College helped me understand the scientific method better. I now believe that the scientific method is the best tool we have in distinguishing fact from fantasy, truth from fiction. We have much left to learn about our world, but we learn more every day.

§

Many years of slow change until I decided to confront my religious beliefs head on. Study of logic, the scientific method, philosophy and psychology all pushed me away from religion

§

Too much of the bible was just not supportable in view of the science. The more I learned of science, the less that the bible could be accepted as anything more than interesting stories. As the religion I was in was very much in the literal tradition, the tension was very high. The change occurred over several years and was relatively painful. In the end, science (defined here as believing the evidence of our eyes but, of course, having much more stringent definitions) could not be denied.

§

Bart Ehrman's books made me agnostic. Reading/watching about the real origins of the earth and universe, made me see that there is no need for a god.

§

We were taught that science was the devil's way of tricking us, and I believed it.

§

Once I came to understand the bible was largely fictional, it wasn't a hard leap to a purely scientific view of the universe.

§

Science was a better path to understand reality. The lack of capacity for the Bible/ Christian faith to account for reality was initially framed as a shortcoming of the believer (or doubter). Eventually facts became too stunningly clear and in contradiction to my belief system.

§

During my first few years of college, even in a Christian fundamentalist institution, I began to question the discrepancies between scientific explanations and religious tales. This only snowballed as I entered a non-religious college to finish my studies.

§

I loved science as a child and always had a difficult time reconciling my religion with what I loved so much. I wouldn't allow myself to learn about evolution because I felt too guilty. Once I actually allowed myself to read about it and other theories like it my eyes were opened and I felt foolish for not giving other viewpoints a chance. I also felt foolish that I thought things like "No way I came from a monkey. That sounds too ridiculous. We all know that God created Adam out of dirt."

§

I think the major impetus was reading Carl Sagan's "Demon Haunted World"

§

Reading Sagan and early Dawkins (The Selfish Gene) were major influences.

Question 23: If increased understanding of science and the reliability thereof in ascertaining truth about the natural world were contributing factors in the process of rejecting Christian faith and adopting agnosticism / atheism, how important a role did this play?						
Formerly →	All Respondents Except CEF Christians N=1170	Easter-Christmas Christian, with Some Sunday Schooling N=468	Devout Liberal-Moderate Catholic N=262	Devout Conservative Catholic N=75	Devout Liberal-Moderate Protestant N=365	Devout CEF Protestant N=391
Very important	48.5%	52.6%	46.6%	34.7%	47.4%	48.8%
Somewhat important	23.4%	23.1%	22.9%	22.7%	24.4%	26.9%
Not that important	11.5%	10.3%	10.7%	17.3%	12.3%	9.7%
Not part of the process	16.7%	14.1%	19.8%	25.3%	15.9%	14.6%

Question 24: When you were Christian (before the deconversion process commenced), what was your general political viewpoint?

Formerly →	All Respondents Except CEF Christians N=1170	Easter-Christmas Christian, with Some Sunday Schooling N=468	Devout Liberal-Moderate Catholic N=262	Devout Conservative Catholic N=75	Devout Liberal-Moderate Protestant N=365	Devout CEF Protestant N=391
Very liberal	9.9%	9.2%	14.5%	0.0%	9.6%	1.8%
Liberal	33.4%	35.5%	39.3%	8.0%	31.8%	6.1%
Moderate / Centrist	34.3%	37.4%	31.7%	25.3%	34%	19.7%
Conservative	19.1%	15.2%	13.0%	46.7%	23%	38.9%
Very conservative	3.2%	2.8%	1.5%	20.0%	1.6%	33.5%

Question 25: How do you describe your political views now?

Formerly →	All Respondents Except CEF Christians N=1170	Easter-Christmas Christian, with Some Sunday Schooling N=468	Devout Liberal-Moderate Catholic N=262	Devout Conservative Catholic N=75	Devout Liberal-Moderate Protestant N=365	Devout CEF Protestant N=391
Very liberal	35.3%	32.7%	37.4%	29.3%	38.4%	35.8%
Liberal	38.5%	38.2%	40.5%	29.3%	39.2%	31.2%
Moderate / Centrist	22.4%	25.6%	18.7%	33.3%	18.6%	28.1%
Conservative	3.3%	3.2%	1.9%	8.0%	3.6%	3.8%
Very conservative	0.5%	0.2%	1.5%	0.0%	0.3%	1.0%

Question 26: If your political views changed during your years as a Christian and leading up to your deconversion, what was the impetus for that change, how difficult was that change, over how long a period did the change occur, and what did you end up believing politically? Please use as much space as you wish.

Selected Responses[54] of Respondents Identifying as Formerly Conservative / Evangelical / Fundamentalist (CEF) Protestant (257 of 391 submitted a written response):

I deconverted in the mid 1980's. Politics were less intertwined with evangelical Christianity at that time, and I was less tuned in to politics then. It was not the issue for me then that I imagine it would be for many deconverting Christians now.

§

My political views changed because I stopped accepting what I was told to believe and started thinking for myself and came to my own conclusions.

§

My change from conservative to liberal occurred as I became more independent and politically and culturally aware. The change was difficult due to my parents' continuing conservative views, and I would now call myself an open-minded liberal

§

Moving from very conservative to very liberal took years and was mostly the cause of the failure of a thirty-year marriage. The change was very difficult since I was starting to believe things that no one in my family believed. I am the only one who isn't right-wing Republican and I am estranged from the

---

[54] Represented here are thirteen of forty-two (13 of 42) pages submitted in the FCNA Survey. Submissions in **bold** were cited, in whole or in part, in the text of the paper. Printed here as submitted.

family now. If I told them I was atheist, too, they'd probably stone me.

§

I don't really get involved in politics except in some social issues: my views on abortion and gay rights pretty much turned around completely. Gay rights was a very slow process, by degrees, and took years, starting when I was in high school and discovered that I had gay friends, and spanning all the way into college when I actually thought about and researched things like gay adoption and gay relationship studies, and found them to be just as legitimate as heterosexual ones. It also had to do with discovering my own sexuality (asexuality) and realizing that if I could think so differently than most of the population, then why were homosexual leanings any less valid?

§

I couldn't go along with church-advocated discrimination against gays and lesbians.

§

Once I realized the Bible is wrong about a lot of things that took away most of my motives for being conservative. When the Bible wasn't doing my thinking for me I arrived at different answers.

§

I wasn't really very politically minded as a Christian. Now I consider myself a freethinker, not really aligning with either major party. I tend to vote democratic nowadays just to avoid having right-wing fundamentalists in office.

§

I had been a Republican because I thought it was the only thing a real Christian could do. I followed Pat Robertson and John Hagee and such people (though it can be so embarrassing to admit it). I remember watching Pat Robertson say God told him George Bush senior would be re-elected. I remember that not happening. When I could no longer believe Christianity, I actually had the wonderful experience of thinking through my own reasoning, morality, and politics for the first time.

§

I was programmed into Christianity just as much as being programmed to be a conservative Republican as a child. Both went together hand-in-hand. Conservative politics and evangelical Christianity meshed within the congregation. My politics began to change before my deconversion and actually changed more since my deconversion.

§

My political views changed as my ethical views changed. My ethical views changed as I realized the Bible and my prescribed religion were immoral in many ways.

§

The biggest change was that I met, and became fond of, several gay people, and as I got to know them I realized that they had no choice at all - they were born as they were. Either God made them gay just to condemn them for it, or there was some other reason.

§

I was a typical religious right member. Before I started drifting from Christianity I started moving closer to the center upon accepting that my actual understanding of the issues was lacking. Took a couple years. After questioning my way out of Christianity I thought it was only wise to honestly listen to the left leaning ideas I had rejected so vehemently and moved to libertarianism, then started to even accept the economic attitudes that get you branded as a "liberal."

§

After several years of therapy I realized that my conservative beliefs stemmed from the negative emotions that had built up over so many years in a fundamentalist environment. When those emotions disappeared I felt no affinity for conservatism at all. In fact, the thought of it makes me nauseous.

§

As a Christian I was an ultra conservative who was pro-life and anti-gay marriage because that's what I was taught to believe. Now I am a libertarian who is socially liberal and fiscally conservative.

§

I was very conservative in my politics largely because of those around me. I listened to sermons on sexual immorality during the Clinton/Lewinsky scandal and heard talk radio sing praises of George W. Bush. Abortion was evil. Gays were living in sin. I think my socially liberal leanings came out during my teen years (deconversion started at 12). The more people I met and the more experiences I had made me rethink my politics.

§

Centrally, the political shift functioned as a direct positive inverse correlation with my shift from Biblical literalism to symbolism, and more so from theism itself to non-theism.

§

During my teenage years at a Christian school, my political beliefs fell in line with that of my church and school, and those beliefs could be described as almost militantly conservative.

§

This was a much more radical shift that occurred much more quickly. It wasn't difficult, however. My studying of the teachings of Christ in-depth revealed the contradictions that exist in Conservative politics.

§

I struggled with conservative Christian viewpoints and eventually came to realize that I did not share the same political sensibilities as the rest of the congregation.

§

Like religion, my political views were given to me via childhood indoctrination. It wasn't until I realized that I had no idea what I actually believed for myself that I took the time to study it out and form opinions of my own....My religious beliefs kept my political opinions in check. It wasn't until I had rejected my faith that my political views shifted dramatically.

§

A big factor was being female and bisexual. I couldn't accept that I was less important than a man, or that my feelings for other girls were unnatural.

§

Was very conservative only because of the influence of my social circles. Upon further reflection and maturing, my views moderated. Paralleled my de-conversion (for many of the same reasons) but not connected.

§

Our church actively encouraged us to vote Republican (pro-life, anti-gay, etc.) We prayed for politicians. I can remember going through a Rush Limbaugh phase in high school. But I think that I just accepted conservative views because I grew up with them. I was not challenged on those views until I got older and actually met gay people and actually had a pregnancy scare myself and considered abortion. When my church prayed the demon of feminism out of me, I really took a second look. I guess you could say that "real life" happened and I realized that my conservative stances were ridiculous. As an adult I look back and realize that the church's intolerance was probably one of the first things to put me off. Now, my husband is a pro-choice libertarian. I find his arguments to be well-thought-out and reasonable. But I would classify myself more as a centrist. I like many libertarian ideas, but still feel more strongly about having a social safety net than my husband. I feel very ignorant of history and politics; I'm still learning. I would say that my political beliefs are continuing to evolve.

§

My political view changes were mostly from listening to my father, who is an extreme conservative, continue to rant and rave. He was so extreme and rude that it made me question everything he said. Also, the fact that most conservatives base their views completely on their religion began to turn me away from that belief system.

§

For a while I bought into the Christianizing of America platform, then rejected that even before I rejected Christianity - I didn't see it as a truly Biblical notion. Before I rejected Christianity and shortly after I figured politics should largely be neutral to a variety of moral issues. Now that I'm distanced from Christianity I think that the political system should be active in bringing about a flourishing society in which as many members as possible have the best life possible, as this is the only life we live.

§

The biggest change may have also had to do with the ever increasing tendency of conservative candidates being religiously biased in their worldview, inhibiting human rights, environmental policy and foreign relations, the belief in a higher power clouds their judgment and puts the entire world at risk.

§

This is probably the most important piece of my removal from faith. I cannot stomach the way people have taken religion to hateful extremes.

§

9-11-2001 was the turning point and helped push me over the hump to deconversion. I could not believe the crap that spilled from the mouths of the likes of Jerry Falwell and Pat Robertson, just to name a few, blaming everyone but the terrorists who committed the murders. Churches initiated what amounted to hate campaigns against homosexuals and nonbelievers. I had been a Republican prior to 9-11 and now I am non partisan in politics but vote mostly Democratic. I'll never vote conservative again. Republicans appear to be owned by the Christian church and have no vision for America.

§

Raised Republican, I was staunch conservative. When I stopped believing that God had a hand in earthly matters, my political views became slowly more and more liberal. I only voted for Bush once.

§

As I grew more and more distant from religion, I became more and more liberal. It was not a difficult change--it was very gradual. I think that coming to accept that homosexuality is not evil was the primary impetus for my losing religion. When I was an adolescent, I was very conservative, by the time I was in high school I was vaguely moderate, leaning toward libertarian. When I was in college I started out vaguely libertarian, leaning toward liberal. And now I would consider myself liberal.

§

I was a conservative Republican (as my family is) for a long time, but actually became a bit of a leftie as a result of reading Scripture (Sermon on the Mount, Acts, the Minor Prophets). I'm now more centrist.

§

Realizing that conservative Christian views are not truly compassionate about the plight of humanity for its own sake. I found secular humanism more in line with my new outlook.

§

My political beliefs were one of the last hold outs of my time as a Christian because my secular beliefs were so tied to Christian principals and I [held] to them in the psychologically turbulent time of my conversion.

§

This change has taken even longer in some regards. Once I dropped my fundamentalist perspective I slowly began to address each issue individually rather than ideologically...While I do consider myself extremely progressive, I tend to be more of a moderate on economic issues and extremely liberal on social issues.

§

This was one of the biggest factors in my deconversion as all the Christians I knew kept taking regressive positions, like they wanted Christianity taught in public schools or didn't think non-Christians should be able to vote.

§

My religious beliefs had nothing to do with my political views. I have always believed in voting for the individual and not for a party. I had always voted a split ticket. The last 4 1/2 years have altered my thinking. I have witnessed unbelievable unfair attacks on a decent human being. I have watched a Congress bent on the same man's total destruction. I have seen members of my own family alienated one from the other due to the unreasonable fears that have been sown in their hearts and souls against this man. I believe that we have to fight against the purveyors of these fears and falsehoods. We cannot allow them to succeed in their efforts.

§

I realised that most socially conservative positions were informed by literalist interpretations of the Bible, and they started seeming more and more silly as my understanding of the Bible changed. Shamefully, I must admit that I went through a college libertarian phase, but overall my political beliefs have become more nuanced with age. I tend to be fairly moderate to left-leaning on most things now.

§

Most of the impetus was from how Christians treated gays and how Christians wanted more church/state integration. The change was very gradual and I'm trying very hard to separate religion from political stances (except for theocracy) when at all possible.

§

No change, except that my views on religion make it more difficult to associate with the Republican party, which I view as being more explicitly "for Christians."

§

Politics really did not play a part in my deconversion. I became more liberal after my deconversion was mostly complete, as I met friends who were more liberal.

§

My political views did not change so much during my years as a Christian as afterwards. During my Christian years I was a socially conservative Republican, though I was never quite as rabid about it as some. My moral metric did shift after my deconversion, which contributed to my becoming more socially liberal, though I think that growing older and becoming more educated also contributed.

§

Politics were a big thing at church. Rejecting one meant rejecting the other, my political shift occurred with my deconversion

§

I was always liberal and believed in civil rights for all and always found the Christian stand against gay marriage and birth control and abortion to be offensive and ignorant. I would turn a blind ear to it when the pastor would preach about it and I've always regretted it.

§

I was very conservative growing up, my family frequently listened to Rush Limbaugh and the like. I believed everything I was told, and thought that Fox News was awesome. "Thank God we have a conservative voice in the media." I vividly remember throwing a pillow at the TV because Bill Clinton was talking and I couldn't stand it. I also remember my pastor encouraging everyone to vote for Bush and praying that God would watch over his campaign so we could have a godly man in the President's office.

§

My political views changed more as a result of George W. Bush than anything related to religion.

§

Discovering political ideas outside of those I was raised with did factor into my de-conversion.

§

Les Miserables, East of Eden, Swing Kids were the primary changers of my political paradigm. I saw the compassion I saw in Jesus in the characters in Hugo's masterpiece, and I did not see that compassion in the Conservatives I knew. East of Eden helped me recognize a lot of perceptual relativism. Swing Kids made me feel I was raised in a neo-nazi cult, there were so many things about the Hitler Youth that reminded me of Neo-Pentecostal programs I had been in, that it utterly beat it out of me.

§

Losing my religion forced me to reevaluate all of my beliefs that were based on my religious beliefs, including my political beliefs. With no god dictating from on high, and no end-times prophecy dooming us, humans actually have the potential to make our planet into a peaceful, pleasant place to live. I was already traveling to the Left on the political spectrum in the years before my deconversion, but it sealed the deal and placed me firmly in the Liberal camp.

§

I would say that political/social issues was a much larger player in my deconversion than anything else.

§

I was a vocal Christian conservative throughout college, but soon began to see that the world was much more complex than I had thought, and that the viewpoints of those who influenced me were hot air, and they were generally fucking idiots. As I studied philosophy, I began to develop a finer sense of compassion. I am now a democratic socialist.

§

My political views were very much like my grandmother's, and my father's. I think the change took place over a decade or so of chipping away at them. Since I have changed from a Christian viewpoint to a more secular morality, I have found I can no longer harbor ideas that are opposed to the goodwill of my fellow humans.

§

It took about 10 years for my political views to do a complete reversal. Mostly it was just getting out of the church cocoon and meeting different people through school activities and eventually going to college and getting a job. I moved two states away from my parents, so their conservative views really didn't influence me anymore. I eventually came to settle into fairly liberal views.

§

When I understood the Bible was not divine truth, I began to understand how religion was used to guide social policy. This began my drift toward liberal politics.

§

Well, politics were spewed from the pulpit. My parents were conservative, the church I grew up with was conservative so I had no other influence. It wasn't until I started to mature emotionally as a teenager that I began to have a difference of opinion.

§

I hated hating people.

§

Once I recognized that a great deal of conservative belief was based in Biblical teachings, and I came to see those teaching as based in Bronze Age understandings of the world, it was easy to discard the whole belief system.

§

Part of it was that I was raised in the South around very conservative, religious people, and moving away from that environment helped me to think more clearly about things for myself...It was a very much "group mentality" and I never thought about dissenting from the perspective of my peers, family members, and those I looked up to. As I got older, I started to think for myself more, research, question, learn, and form my own opinions.

§

As stated, there were slow changes towards being liberal as I became aware of the inconsistencies of religion and the harm it was causing on those who did not question. Decided that religion did not respect the rights of all humans and was not truly compassionate

§

I found as I learned more about other cultures, religions, and human rights my political leanings naturally migrated to the liberal end of the spectrum.

§

My views change fairly quickly after losing the faith. Religion held my views to the right.

§

I think once I grasped the concept of there being no hell, no heaven, no one watching and constantly judging, my conservative views really started to slough off. I would still describe myself as a fiscal conservative, but once I realized that all the social issues I thought should follow the Bible were really a private and not public matter, I became more a centrist.

§

My new way of thinking gradually changed my political point of view. I went, over the course of a few years from hard core conservative to far left.

§

I had become socially liberal, mostly, slightly before deconverting. After I lost my religion, I became more liberal.

§

I was very conservative, I thought that all the signs of the Bible pointed to a conservatism type of society. I ended up going very far Left, it wasn't difficult.

§

My original political views were very conservative because that was the only acceptable viewpoint in my organization and my family. When I became freed to think for myself I became much more liberal and generally more supportive of individual rights. This transformation took from 5-10 years.

§

My politics are the same economically, but many things have changed for me in other areas because of my deconversion. I no longer follow Biblical mandates and therefore no longer place any judgment on homosexuals. I am furthermore ashamed and horrified that I ever believed otherwise. I also no longer believe that there is a conspiracy against Christians, that there is a "liberal media" out to get everyone, or that prayer should be in schools. I am overall a less-judgmental and a more compassionate person.

§

I became a more caring, compassionate, respectful, and progressive person after deconverting.

Question 27: If adopting political views that were more moderate or liberal than those of your church was a contributing factor in the process of rejecting Christian faith and adopting agnosticism / atheism, how important a role did this play?

Formerly →	All Respondents Except CEF Christians =1170	Easter-Christmas Christian, with Some Sunday Schooling N=468	Devout Liberal-Moderate Catholic N=262	Devout Conservative Catholic N=75	Devout Liberal-Moderate Protestant N=365	Devout CEF Protestant N=391
Very important	11.5%	8.5%	13.4%	16.0%	12.9%	13.6%
Somewhat important	17.2%	17.9%	16.0%	8.0%	18.9%	24.0%
Not that important	19.9%	18.8%	18.3%	14.7%	23.6%	19.9%
Not part of the process	51.5%	54.7%	52.3%	61.3%	44.7%	42.5%

Question 28: For whom did you vote in the 2008 presidential election?

Formerly →	All Respondents Except CEF Christians N=1170	Easter-Christmas Christian, with Some Sunday Schooling N=468	Devout Liberal-Moderate Catholic N=262	Devout Conservative Catholic N=75	Devout Liberal-Moderate Protestant N=365	Devout CEF Protestant N=391
Obama / Biden	63.6%	60.3%	66.0%	54.7%	67.9%	60.9%
McCain / Palin	3.9%	3.0%	4.2%	8.0%	4.1%	7.4%
Did not vote / Other[55]	32.5%	36.8%	29.8%	37.3%	27.9%	31.7%

Data for those who were eligible to vote in 2008 (U.S. citizen, at least 18), did vote, and voted for one of the two major party candidates (1057 respondents):

Formerly →	All Respondents Except CEF Christians N=790	Former Devout CEF Christians N=257
Obama / Biden	94.2%	89.1%
McCain / Palin	5.8%	10.9%

---

[55] The "Did not vote / Other" category includes non-U.S. citizens and U.S. citizens who did not vote and U.S. citizens who voted for other candidates, such as Bob Barr (Libertarian), Ralph Nader (Independent), and Ron Paul (write-in).

Question 29: For whom will you vote in the 2012 presidential election?						
Formerly →	All Respondents Except CEF Christians	Easter-Christmas Christian, with Some Sunday Schooling N=468	Devout Liberal-Moderate Catholic N=262	Devout Conservative Catholic N=75	Devout Liberal-Moderate Protestant N=365	Devout CEF Protestant N=391
Barack Obama	59.8%	60.0%	63.0%	44%	60.5%	60.6%
Republican nominee	5.3%	5.3%	5.0%	10.7%	4.4%	5.9%
Will not vote / Other[56]	34.9%	34.6%	32.1%	45.3%	35.1%	33.5%

Data for those who will be eligible to vote in 2012 (U.S. citizen, at least 18), intend to vote, and will vote for one of the two major party candidates (1057 respondents):

Formerly →	All Respondents Except CEF Christians N=762	Former Devout CEF Christians N=260
Obama / Biden	91.9%	91.2%
GOP Candidate	8.1%	8.8%

---

[56] The "Will not vote/Other" category includes non-U.S. citizens, U.S. citizens who do not plan to vote, and U.S. citizens who remain undecided or will vote for other candidates, such as Ralph Nader ("if he runs"), Ron Paul ("if he runs Libertarian").

Question 30: When you were Christian (before the deconversion process commenced), what were your views about homosexuality?

Formerly →	All Respondents Except CEF Christians N=1170	Easter-Christmas Christian, with Some Sunday Schooling N=468	Devout Liberal-Moderate Catholic N=262	Devout Conservative Catholic N=75	Devout Liberal-Moderate Protestant N=365	Devout CEF Protestant N=391
Very liberal and accepting	21.0%	25.2%	24.0%	8.0%	16.2%	3.8%
Liberal and accepting	24.0%	24.4%	26.7%	6.7%	25.2%	9.2%
Moderate / Centrist, not sure what I thought	32.3%	30.8%	30.2%	25.3%	37.3%	24.0%
Conservative and uncomfortable	20.3%	18.2%	17.6%	52.0%	18.4%	43.7%
Very conservative (knew all the "clobber-verses" by heart and believed them)	2.4%	1.5%	1.5%	8.0%	3.0%	19.2%

Question 30 (responses by sexual orientation): When you were Christian (before the deconversion process commenced), what were your views about homosexuality?

	Exclusively Heterosexual N=1024	Primarily Heterosexual N=325	Bisexual N=97	Primarily homosexual N=35	Exclusively homosexual N=64	Asexual N=16
Very liberal and accepting	15.0%	18.2%	22.7%	8.6%	26.6%	37.5%
Liberal and accepting	20.6%	23.1%	13.4%	17.1%	14.1%	18.8%
Moderate / Centrist, not sure what I thought	30.8%	32.0%	26.8%	34.3%	18.8%	18.8%
Conservative and uncomfortable	27.4%	20.9%	25.8%	34.3%	29.7%	18.8%
Very conservative (knew all the "clobber-verses" by heart and believed them)	6.2%	5.8%	11.3%	5.7%	10.9%	6.3%

Question 31: How would you describe your views about homosexuality now?

Formerly →	All Respondents Except CEF Christians N=1170	Easter-Christmas Christian, with Some Sunday Schooling N=468	Devout Liberal-Moderate Catholic N=262	Devout Conservative Catholic N=75	Devout Liberal-Moderate Protestant N=365	Devout CEF Protestant N=391
Very liberal and accepting	77.4%	75.0%	80.2%	77.3%	78.6%	81.1%
Liberal and accepting	20.1%	22.2%	17.2%	21.3%	19.2%	14.8%
Moderate / Centrist, not sure what I think	1.9%	2.1%	1.5%	1.3%	1.9%	3.1%
Conserva-tive and uncomfort-able	0.4%	0.4%	0.8%	0.0%	0.3%	1.0%
Very conserva-tive (know all the "clobber-verses" by heart and still believe them)	0.2%	0.2%	0.4%	0.0%	0.0%	0.0%

Question 31 (responses by sexual orientation): How would you describe your views about homosexuality now?						
	Exclusively Heterosexual N=1024	Primarily Heterosexual N=325	Bisexual N=97	Primarily homosexual N=35	Exclusively homosexual N=64	Asexual N=16
Very liberal and accepting	72.9%	84.9%	93.8%	94.3%	96.9%	87.5%
Liberal and accepting	23.3%	13.5%	5.2%	2.9%	3.1%	12.5%
Moderate / Centrist, not sure what I think	2.7%	1.5%	0.0%	2.9%	0.0%	0.0%
Conservative and uncomfortable	0.9%	0.0%	0.0%	0.0%	0.0%	0.0%
Very conservative (know all the "clobber-verses" by heart and still believe them)	0.1%	0.0%	1.0%	0.0%	0.0%	0.0%

Question 32: If your views about homosexuality changed during your years as a Christian and leading up to your deconversion, what was the impetus for that change, how difficult was that change, over how long a period did that change occur, and what did you end up believing about homosexuality? Please use as much space as you wish.

Selected Responses[57] of Respondents Identifying as Formerly Conservative / Evangelical / Fundamentalist Protestant (272 of 391 submitted a written response).

Knowing homosexuals personally changed my view of them.

§

As a Christian, it would probably be fair to say I hated homosexuals to some degree. I was taught disregard for gays, and I used my religion to justify how I felt.

§

My views didn't change until after I had deconverted. I once believed it was wrong because I was told to believe that. Now I see that these are people that are being discriminated against just as other races and women were before them.

§

As I grew older (14-16 years old) I got a strong feeling that all desires are equal and I started to develop a strong doubt in the Bible's views on non-heterosexuality and especially what people in my church where saying about it.

§

I struggled with the way my faith was making me act like a jerk.

---

[57] Represented here are ten of forty-five (10 of 45) pages submitted in the FCNA Survey. Submissions in **bold** were cited, in whole or in part, in the text of the paper. Printed here as submitted.

§

I always knew I was attracted to women, and it was agony for an outsider homeschooled smart-but-awkward kid to put all my life's purpose and work into something that told me over and over that I was somehow horribly flawed. I tried to see counselors, to talk to people, to pray away the gay, as they say, but it didn't work, and the process horrified and disgusted me....Honestly, losing religion was such a weight off my young shoulders. Suddenly I wasn't a freak and a sinner, doomed to a vice I couldn't seem to shake, but instead I was a normal young person who fell in a normal spectrum of human behavior, accepted by sociologists and psychiatrists and other scientists worldwide.

§

When my belief in Christianity was gone, I had to examine issues based on other reasons, not being told any more what I should think. I read that homosexuality occurred in nature, I made friends with homosexuals (for the first time) in college (after my first degree), I read about important homosexual and bisexual people in history, esp. in Greek and Roman history. I no longer had any reason to condemn homosexuals, and I saw that the homosexuals I knew did not chose to be homosexual, they simply were what they were. That gelled with my other observations that desires are experienced, not really chosen. I ended up accepting homosexuality and bisexuality, even though I am basically heterosexual.

§

My views on homosexuality were a defining moment in my deconversion.

§

It's another example where I found the Christian religion and the Bible to be immoral.

§

I never had anything against gays. I knew the clobber verses but only accepted them reluctantly because I couldn't stomach what I thought would be disagreeing with god. I voted to amend my state constitution to prevent gay marriage because I saw it as voicing my approval or disapproval as part of the community; it put me on the wrong side of history and I regret it with my whole heart.

§

As a Southern Baptist, sex was a taboo subject. One of the church secretaries had been married to another church member, and came to her wedding night a virgin. He told her that God had spoken to him and told him that he was to keep her "pure," so the marriage was never consummated. Four years later, she caught him in bed with another man, and the church closed ranks around her. This didn't sit well with me. What her husband did was wrong, but not for the reasons the church said. I began to question the church's stand on homosexuality, and had several friends who were gay. The more research I did, the more I was convinced that homosexuality was not unnatural, and my existing doubts about the validity of the Bible only reinforced my belief that the church was wrong to condemn it.

§

I had a very intelligent friend who was a homosexual, and the more I got to know him, the harder it was for me to think of him as "hellbound."

§

The emotional-cultural prejudice here went deeper than the cognitive aspect of the "clobber verses" (Very accurate phrase!). Accordingly, this change was one of the last to fall. Here science specifically helped, as I learned more and more of how homosexuality has a certain percentage found throughout in nature. It's (DUH) *natural*—well-documented in some 400+ species, as I understand it.)

§

I have never been strongly homophobic although my religious leaders were. The awakening process requires a review of all beliefs, but not just a review, a personal challenge to them. I have good friends now who are lbgt. I strongly compare atheism to being lbgt because we are equally discriminated against.

§

This was the main reason I left the church and de-converted. Given the beliefs I had, I couldn't imagine being gay and Christian. Although I began having sexual thoughts of a homosexual nature by age 13 or 14, I repressed them to the best of my ability and hoped they would go away. Denying my sexuality was very, very difficult. Now I'm a proud gay man, but very resentful of my Christian upbringing.

§

I had a lot of anxiety in my early adolescence due to my bisexual urges and my church and family's very clear hatred of homosexuality.

§

My church's stance on homosexuality was one of the first things that really came to bother me. I met a gay classmate in high school. I found that he had the same issues and same experiences with his partner that I had with my boyfriend. He clearly loved in the same way that I did. I saw nothing wrong with his behavior and feelings, and I couldn't understand what was so bad. After meeting him I immediately rejected my church's stance on homosexuality. I actually became angered by it. My father was, and continues to be, seriously homophobic. It divides us still. I believe churches should be pro-love and pro-marriage. I cannot understand the hatred toward LGBT. My husband's sister is gay. Voting pro-gay is very important to me as an adult.

§

I knew what the Christian community taught me about homosexuality, and I was uncomfortable with it because I felt like it dehumanized anyone "different."

§

By ultimately dismissing the Bible as any kind of authority on matters of sexuality, I simply had no basis to oppose/condemn homosexuality. Over the years I have come to know more and more people who manifest same-sex attraction, and it just became obvious that it was normal in a given population.

§

My first husband was gay and died from AIDS. Had the church not forced him into a shameful role, he might still be alive today.

§

This issue was a pretty big factor in my deconversion. Why would god create homosexuals? It didn't make any sense.

§

I sat in church one Sunday and the pastor called homosexuals an abomination in the eyes of God. It ripped my heart to shreds, as I saw the face of each and every one of my homosexual friends flash through my mind. I thought to myself, how dare you! How dare you sit in judgment of your fellow human beings!...I couldn't justify aligning myself with his view of homosexuals, and this played a massive part in my deconversion

§

The change in my views on homosexuality came from rejecting most of the "pulpit teachings" and trappings of morality as taught by churches/religion. I could evaluate on my own what I thought about activities, and came to the "golden rule" conclusion: consensual activity between adults is a good thing. Love is love. Lust is lust. All are part of the human experience.

§

I became uncomfortable towards the end of my Christianity with the fervor and hatred Christians had towards homosexuals.

§

This was probably the starting point of my losing religion. I came to accept my being gay, and knew that any religion that condemns it is not the religion for me. I first accepted that I was gay when I was in 6th grade. I knew something was "wrong." I prayed daily for God to make me straight. By the time I was 14, I knew it wasn't going away, and I started to grow to accept it. The more I accepted it and realized it was natural and perfectly harmless to be gay, the more ridiculous Christianity seemed.

§

As with evolution, it was a relief to not have to hold traditional Christian views of homosexuality.

§

This is a place in which I didn't get along with most other Christians. I have always been accepting of homosexuals and most Christians here (West Michigan) aren't, despite the Christian teaching of "love thy neighbor." This obscene self-contradiction was another reason I rejected Christianity.

§

The absolute reason for my religious fundamentalism as well as my religious deconversion was the fact that I am gay. I am the epitome of a person who "protests too much." I truly believed that one could pray the gay away if they had enough faith... I, of course, just didn't have enough faith!

§

If I had to pick a single cause for my de-conversion, this would be it. While my church taught the "hate the sin, love the sinner" line, in practice there was a lot of open bigotry, not just condescension. It also became clear to me that gay people weren't defying God to get back at him for an unhappy childhood, but really didn't think being gay was wrong. It hardly seemed fair of God to set us up with a conscience that told us his religion was wrong, then required us to correctly guess which religion was right based on rather weak evidence and no internal compulsion, with eternal punishment if we guessed wrong.

§

This hits close to home. I actually am gay. I always denied it and was afraid to come out. I believed it was wrong because of what the Bible said. I struggled a very long time with this. I eventually came out to my friends in college.

§

Again, same thing. I used to be an ignorant, racist, homophobic jackass. All it took was some education and rational thought to change my mind. I hate, and am embarrassed by, who I used to be.

§

I am bisexual. My first crush was a same sex crush when I was in third grade. As I developed sexually, I was drawn to people of the same sex first. **The single biggest issue in my rejecting Christianity was knowing full well that I, in my natural state, was bisexual. If I was created deliberately by god, why would he create someone he would hate? Once you step outside and look at it, the Christian mythos falls apart.**

§

All the scientific studies showing it is determined. Later, reading the OT and seeing how Christians cherry pick a few verses while ignoring all the more uncomfortable rules and laws that no one in their right mind would follow.

§

One of the things I'm most ashamed of today -- Though I de-converted in my late teens, I was outspokenly anti-gay from around puberty until then. Granted, it was mostly posturing and trying to act "macho" around my peers, but the Bible and religion played directly into it. It wasn't really until college that I got to know more gay people and began to realize how hurtful my words/beliefs must have been.

§

This was a major factor in my deconversion. At the start of my deconversion, along with OT violence and the Genesis story, I struggled with the Bible's condemnation of homosexuality.... I was unable to reconcile my feelings with what I knew the Bible said. My foundation was shaky after reading about all of God's early genocides and infanticides, and when I started to play with the idea that the Bible might not be true, the homosexuality problem was one of the first major things I realized made a lot more sense outside of a Christian worldview.

§

Prior to my de-conversion, I was confused. I was told time and again how disgusting it was. I was taught "don't hate the sinner, hate the sin" but I thought how can you separate a person from their sexuality? And what was wrong with it anyway? I met people who were gay in college, and it confused me because.... they were NOT evil! They were like anyone else. I didn't see any reason to say that there was anything wrong with them. They were just...themselves.

§

It was not until the final deconversion at age 29 that the last of my bigotry toward homosexuality fell away. It had been a gradual process since 15, but it was not until the end that the last of it went, and good riddance.

§

I was a hater. Now I'm not. I'm better now that I quit religion.

§

This is a view I couldn't justify outside of my beliefs. This took over a year and was a key to my rejecting the rest of my beliefs

§

I am gay, and that had a big impact on my de-conversion.

§

My whole worldview shifted in college as I had more time away from the church, and more discussions with classmates and friends.

§

I am gay, I have been aware of my sexuality since I was a child. My immediate family was very accepting and even most of my extended family. Not all but most. In fact my homosexuality is nowhere near as much a problem as my atheism. I cannot emphasize that enough. My atheism is far, far morbid an issue with my family than my being gay. The two are not even close.

§

There's no place to learn hate like a Sunday school classroom....Gays were simply not tolerated during my childhood.

§

In spite of my fundamentalism, I couldn't hate gay people and often defended them, leading my fundamentalist friends to wonder if I was secretly gay. (I am not.) Realizing that the Bible was never inspired lifted the weight off me and I no longer felt obligated to do those damn mental gymnastics.

§

I am a gay man and initially accepted my church's teachings. However as I learned about queer history, especially as it related to the early Christian church, I came to see scripture as either politically motivated, or based in bronze age, patriarchal superstitions.

§

This was another factor in my political transition because I saw Republicans as massive hypocrites and full of hatred.

§

Reality trumps myth. Initially my views about homosexuality were based in the Bible's teachings as literal Word of God. Now they are reality-based.

§

I "struggled" with homosexual urges myself. I was sent to a Christian psychologist. It was quite traumatizing.

§

I no longer wanted to be a part of a faith that was so cruel to other human beings.

§

I understand now that it was a bigoted opinion that was heavily informed by my religious views.

§

I realized I was gay at a young age, but religion allowed me to deny and hate myself for a long time. In my early twenties, I came out to myself.

Question 33: If adopting a more tolerant / liberal perspective about homosexuality than that of your church was a contributing factor in the process of rejecting Christian faith and adopting agnosticism / atheism, how important a role did this play?						
Formerly →	All Respondents Except CEF Christians N=1170	Easter-Christmas Christian, with Some Sunday Schooling N=468	Devout Liberal-Moderate Catholic N=262	Devout Conservative Catholic N=75	Devout Liberal-Moderate Protestant N=365	Devout CEF Protestant N=391
Very important	12.0%	9.4%	12.6%	21.3%	12.9%	18.2%
Somewhat important	18.8%	16.7%	19.5%	16.0%	21.6%	18.4%
Not that important	16.8%	17.9%	15.3%	12.0%	17.3%	22.3%
Not part of the process	52.5%	56.0%	52.7%	50.7%	48.2%	41.2%

Question 33 (responses by sexual orientation): If adopting a more tolerant / liberal perspective about homosexuality than that of your church was a contributing factor in the process of rejecting Christian faith and adopting agnosticism / atheism, how important a role did this play?	Exclusively Heterosexual N=1024	Primarily Heterosexual N=325	Bisexual N=97	Primarily homosexual N=35	Exclusively homosexual N=64	Asexual N=16
Very important	8.0%	15.1%	21.6%	37.1%	67.2%	18.8%
Somewhat important	17.7%	22.8%	22.7%	20.0%	7.8%	18.8%
Not that important	19.8%	18.8%	11.3%	5.7%	4.7%	18.8%
Not part of the process	54.5%	43.4%	46.7%	37.1%	20.3%	46.7%

Question 34: How do you define your sexual orientation?

Formerly →	All Respondents Except CEF Christians N=1170	Easter-Christmas Christian, with Some Sunday Schooling N=468	Devout Liberal-Moderate Catholic N=262	Devout Conservative Catholic N=75	Devout Liberal-Moderate Protestant N=365	Devout CEF Protestant N=391
Asexual	0.9%	0.9%	0.8%	1.3%	1.1%	1.3%
Exclusively heterosexual	67.9%	70.5%	63.4%	76%	66%	58.8%
Primarily heterosexual	20.6%	20.9%	22.5%	8.0%	21.4%	21.5%
Bisexual	4.8%	4.5%	6.5%	5.3%	3.8%	10.5%
Primarily homosexual	2.3%	1.5%	2.7%	2.7%	3.0%	2.0%
Exclusively homosexual	3.5%	1.7%	4.2%	6.7%	4.7%	5.9%

Question 35: When you were Christian (before the deconversion process commenced), how did you view life's pain and suffering?						
Formerly →	All Respondents Except CEF Christians N=1170	Easter-Christmas Christian, with Some Sunday Schooling N=468	Devout Liberal-Moderate Catholic N=262	Devout Conservative Catholic N=75	Devout Liberal-Moderate Protestant N=365	Devout CEF Protestant N=391
All pain and suffering was a result of the Fall and human error and would be healed by God in the Kingdom	15.3%	9.4%	11.1%	26.7%	23.6%	46.8%
Some pain and suffering was the result of the Fall and human error and some was God's punishment /	40.5%	37.4%	45.0%	45.3%	40.3%	40.4%
Pain and suffering just were and there was no adequate explanation	44.2%	53.2%	43.9%	28.0%	36.2%	12.8%

Question 36: What are you views about pain and suffering now?						
Formerly →	All Respondents Except CEF Christians N=1170	Easter-Christmas Christian, with Some Sunday Schooling N=468	Devout Liberal-Moderate Catholic N=262	Devout Conservative Catholic N=75	Devout Liberal-Moderate Protestant N=365	Devout CEF Protestant N=391
All pain and suffering was a result of the Fall and human error and would be healed by God in the Kingdom	0.2%	0.2%	0.0%	0.0%	0.3%	0.3%
Some pain and suffering was the result of the Fall and human error and some was God's punishment /	0.6%	0.2%	0.4%	0.0%	1.4%	0.3%
Pain and suffering just were and there was no adequate explanation	99.2%	99.6%	99.6%	100%	98.4%	99.5%

Question 37: If your views about pain and suffering (theodicy) changed during your years as a Christian and leading up to your deconversion, what was the impetus for that change, how difficult was the change, over how long a period did the change occur, and what did you end up believing about pain and suffering? Please use as much space as you wish.

Selected Responses[58] of Respondents Identifying as Formerly Conservative / Evangelical / Fundamentalist Protestant (224 of 391 submitted a written response).

Over the ten or so years it took to change (de-convert), I witnessed many Christians whose suffering made me search the Bible and then rethink my faith and concept of God. I saw no reason for their pain and loss. God's love and empathy dissipated in the presence of their suffering and premature deaths. This was THE issue that weighed heavily upon me. Also, the amount of suffering in the world is too immense to be justified. In the afterlife, Hell makes the world's suffering a pittance in comparison. No God should be so cruel. Pain and suffering are part of life, and we should seek to alleviate them. This proves to me that the Biblegod is a sick fantasy.

§

Ha! Theodicy. I view this as the single most condemning issue concerning the Christian God. The Christian God is supposed to be "the God of love". Allowing cheetahs to eat gazelles while the gazelles are still alive cannot be described as an act of "the God of love". Hence, there are two logical choices: The Christian God does not exist. The Christian God exists but is a monster not worthy of respect by the most depraved criminal.

---

[58] Represented here are fourteen of forty (14 of 40) pages submitted in the FCNA Survey. Submissions in **bold** were cited, in whole or in part, in the text of the paper. Printed here as submitted.

§

If a child gets cancer people start praying for his recovery. If the child survives they say it was a miracle. If the child dies they say he was an angel and god was recalling him home to heaven. Logically, if god was going to cure the boy why did he give him cancer to start with? If the boy dies, does this mean god likes him more or less than the child he decides to let live? One he chooses to call home to heaven, one he lets live and stay on earth. So which one does he like more? Totally illogical.

§

This was most definitely a part of my deconversion. My family was in a car accident and as a result, one of my sons is now paraplegic. I had a very difficult time understanding why and how it happened and why our struggles had to keep on going on year out and year in. We had to fight in court. I had to quit my job. And many other things. My son still suffers medical conditions that threatens his life and the stress is unbearable at times. I feel like I've been to Hell... and stayed there... and will have to stay there until my last breath. And it's even worse for my son. I just can't understand why God would put such a burden on our family.

§

I was deeply disturbed by the weakness of C.S. Lewis' book *The Problem of Pain*. He laid out the problem very clearly, and answered it very poorly. This tops the reasons to disbelieve list.

§

I had a beloved cat die and I was suffering over it and wondered why I could go to heaven and she couldn't. It didn't make sense. Now I know we all cease to exist when we die and there's no rhyme or reason for suffering.

§

I guess the biggest impetus was learning to think logically. Why would a god who knows everything, can do anything, and loves us unconditionally and completely put us in a world where we can be so desperately harmed? Even if it was because of Eve and Adam, it didn't make sense that everyone should be punished for their mistakes (or, indeed, for them to be punished--they didn't know they were doing anything wrong until they'd done it). So I used to think that people sinning was the cause of injustice in an abstract way, but when I actually gave it some thought it didn't make any sense. The belief that bad things are always our fault fell apart with my loss of belief in god.

§

Prayers for a friend who had cancer were not answered (many people prayed). Eventually I came to think that Christianity cannot escape the Problem of Evil.

§

Not only the vast amount of human suffering, but animal suffering, as well. The realization that we cause great harm to our environment. Also, the fact that we are preceded by hundreds of thousands of years of ancestors who lived and died without divine intervention.

§

Logic demonstrates that Christian theology is false regarding the Problem of Evil. The fallacies used by Christian apologetics were a major cause in the death of my faith.

§

When I was 16 I volunteered at a children's hospital. I couldn't understand how God could allow innocent children to suffer. No one could answer this question for me and I began to wonder if there was a God at all.

§

In a nutshell, I can't see how a god would set people up on Earth only to have them suffer so horribly when it knew that would happen. It is sadistic and messed up. I used to think that we were the messed up ones, but throughout my life I gradually realized how insane that was. Suffering sucks, and it happens, and I don't know why. But I also won't pretend that I actually do know why based on no logical reasoning whatsoever.

§

I always found the problem of suffering to be problematic in my beliefs as a Christian and was one of the initial reasons for my doubts which eventually led to my deconversion.

§

I could never get over the suffering of others, which was a big factor to my chronic depression. The whole world was suffering and why couldn't I do anything about it? People can solve issues by just not being selfish. I never understood that and I still don't understand, but the suffering of others really opened my eyes to the awfulness of the Christian god.

§

I could see no reason why a God who loved his creation would torment it in such terrible ways, or allow it to be tormented by other forces in such terrible ways.

§

I was confronted with lots of pain and suffering within my own community and knew that places across the globe were even more worse off. This was the most important factor in my deconversion, and also the most difficult because I spent a couple years trying very hard to reconcile pain and suffering with Christian notions of God. In the end, I could not reconcile this. I believe some pain and suffering is from both natural causes (medical, emotional, etc) and some is from systemic causes (malnutrition, poor public health, exploitation)

§

I felt that much of the emotional suffering I experienced as a Christian was unnecessary, counterproductive, and deliberately brought on by the careless or deliberate actions of my fellow

Christians. This was very important in my decision to leave the church.

§

I started to believe that more pain was caused by faith, and blocking stem cell never made sense to me, even as a devote believer; though I did not argue with my church and stepped in line.

§

God's apparent inability or unwillingness to stop suffering and the idea that He would damn non-believers (or believers of other faiths) who could not possibly be expected to know "The Word" disturbed me greatly. This dilemma was a major factor in my deconversion.

§

In my opinion, the God described in the Abrahamic religions can not logically exist based on what takes place in the world on a daily basis. I don't know, maybe God is just slightly disorganized. I mean, it must be a great deal of work blessing NFL athletes with the gifts needed to perform at that level. He probably just forgot to feed those starving infants in Ethiopia. Also, here is a perfect example of a fundamental contradiction. The Bible describes god as very loving, so much so that we as mere humans could never even attempt to understand. However, God is also vengeful and when he gets pissed bad things happen. Things like genocide on an unbelievable scale. Maybe I am being unreasonable but my definition of love does not include violence in any way, shape or form. *end rant*

§

This happened very gradually over more than a decade. I remember one particular event. I was about 12 years old. My father had been unemployed for some time and our family was seriously struggling. We were living off of charity from the church. He was in line to get a very good job. I prayed and prayed and was sure that God would make this happen for us.

When the job fell through, I was dumbfounded. I believe that's the first time I ever blasphemed.

§

This was something that I used to take solace in. I believed that God would eventually make everything right for everyone. It was hard to lose that belief. Now I feel more social responsibility to make things better for people who cannot help themselves.

§

The problem of evil was critical to my deconversion. I found no adequate explanation -- all the popular ones just seemed transparently bogus.

§

The theodicy issue was certainly one of, if not THE, lynch pins in my de-conversion. I tried to find ways of explaining it, but ultimately the only explanation that satisfies me is an aloof, uncaring god or none at all.

§

On the contrary, this change was very comforting. It was tough to make sense of an omnipotent god who allows so much senseless suffering. The world makes much more sense to me now.

§

I couldn't understand how a loving god could allow some of the atrocities I'd read about. Like the Holocaust. How the hell does he sit by and let that happen?

§

As mentioned above, my own ongoing depression and God's failure to act in response to many years of prayer, deliverance sessions (for casting out demonic spirits), and pleading were the primary causes of my reexamination of this question. I finally concluded that pain and suffering are simply part of the experience of living in an impersonal universe and the way the earth and life evolved.

§

My divorce was the impetus for change. I ended up believing pain and suffering were part of a subjective reality, that we can control our outcomes to an extent and be responsible for our actions toward others morally. I believe human biology carries the diminished traits of evolutionary process still, so we display some caveman like behavior still to this day.

§

This was major in my deconversion. The problem of Job bothered me. If I was distressed by the sufferings of others - how could a loving god not only tolerate it, but bring it about via divine will or plan?

§

This was one of the biggest problems for me as a Christian. I read over 15 books just on this one subject and never found a satisfactory explanation. The suffering of innocent children is unacceptable to me. For a loving God to allow/decree it is unthinkable.

§

Again, studying philosophy and adopting a naturalistic worldview helped here...but particularly, studying Christian apologists such as Augustine and C.S. Lewis and seeing how inadequate their attempts to solve the problem of pain convinced me that it couldn't be reconciled with a omnipotent, omnibenevolent deity.

§

It was a natural extension of my rejection of biblical literalism. It was actually an easy transition for me. My mother died painfully of cancer at the age of 34. As a Christian I had to reconcile this with a loving god, which always made me angry and then guilty for being angry. Once I let go of this idea I could finally accept that my mother simply got sick and died. It was oddly very comforting.

§

My father died when I was 19 years old. That was a time of great spiritual struggle in my life. I also think it played a part in shaking me enough to go and question my religion in a way I never had considered doing prior to that time.

§

I view pain and suffering for the existence of religion in the first place. Life is hard, so to put some meaning in a mystical ideal relieves some of that suffering when you think there is a plan. My take is simple. If you don't want your thumb to hurt, don't hit it with a hammer, but sometimes your thumb may fall under the hammer of someone else.

§

The problem of human suffering gave me the most emotional anguish. I had long been troubled by the pain in my parents' lives (despite their well-lived faith). After I started doubting the Bible, I became much more deeply disturbed by pain and suffering. I had to let go of Heaven, which was one of the most deeply painful aspects of the process. This left me feeling like life was a meaningless collection of painful, pointless years. It took several months for me to begin to discover meaning without God/an afterlife, and I continue to struggle with coping with how painful life really is.

§

Well, when I realized that I had no reason to believe in the bible, and no reason to believe in a deity...I had nothing to rationalize pain and suffering with. I was indoctrinated that because the first humans were tricked into eating a piece of fruit that belonged to their nonmaterial sky daddy...that because of this sneaky snake's cunning influence and a "stupid" woman...the entire future of mankind had to suffer unimaginable pain. I guess that never sat well with me. Oh, and if I could not understand how this could be, it was not for me to understand, because god's ways and thoughts are higher than my own and I couldn't possibly understand at this time...oh and I was supposed to love him for that...

§

I was very influenced by C.S. Lewis, so my views on pain and suffering took a long time to change. Witnessing the death of my mother, watching news footage of atrocious genocides in the world, and seeing good people suffer for no apparent reason definitely started deconverting me. Now, pain and suffering to me is just part of life; sometimes it's caused by our fellow man, and sometimes it's not. We need ethical rules and political policies to minimize it.

§

This was a huge factor for me. It was very difficult for me to harmonize my views about God with the world I observed around me. The impetus for the change was that considering these issues was simply unavoidable for me. This was a life-long issue for me so it took a long time to hash this one out in my head. I used to think God would explain it all to me one day but now I just see pain and suffering as a horrible natural consequence of the world in which we live. There is no cosmic explanation for pain and there will not be a time when it is all made "right" in the future.

§

My mother shocked me one day when she commented that the tsunami of 2004 was the result of sin. Realizing I was completely at odds with my mother and pastors and friends on spiritual topics like this contributed to me realizing I had different views and I inched toward that slippery slope to loss of faith.

§

This was probably one of the more early factors in my questioning of doctrine, but probably not the most important.

§

This was a big one for me, my deconversion occurred after a sermon on why god allows suffering. I was infuriated by the preacher's glibness about those suffering

§

When I was a young woman, I obtained, for reasons both selfish and irresponsible, four abortions from the age of 17 to 23. I straightened up and got married at 29. After 10 years of married childlessness without practicing birth control, I thought I couldn't have any babies and the abortions were the reason/punishment, and I accepted that. Then, just before my 40th birthday, I gave birth to a beautiful, perfect, healthy baby boy. When he was 8 months old, a tsunami swept across Indonesia, and I read about a mother who watched all 11 of her children swept away. I heard a Christian friend of mine say "I just wonder what those people did to incur Gods' wrath like that", and that's when I absolutely knew that there was no god.

§

I could not explain how a supposedly loving god would condemn billions of people to hell who had never even heard the word "Jesus."

§

I think the pain and suffering question for someone in the fold is not a genuine question. It's not realistic to expect a person deeply inside the fold to sense pain and suffering as a question. Though it can start to prompt questions if a lot of it happens to them or a loved one. I felt loved by Jesus. The cosmos was alright by me. I was young and healthy. Pain and suffering grows as a question as one ages perhaps, and after one is no longer in the fold. When you're in the fold it's not too difficult to continue to rationalize away even tremendous pains and suffering of you and your loved ones as a type of "suffering with Christ," "offering it up to Christ." But sometimes the rationalization doesn't work and then the pain and suffering can generate questions.

§

This was probably one of the main driving forces for my deconversion. I guess over a few years I didn't have a clear answer or position on this, but I eventually realised that the "problem of suffering" is insurmountable for a traditional Christian world-view.

§

The impetus was the story of Job. How could a loving god allow the infliction of suffering on an individual to prove his loyalty?

§

I didn't think about it. I just ignored it. There's no way to rationalize it. When I started to think about all the pain and suffering in the world, I couldn't continue believing in a loving God pulling the strings of everything on Earth. That's just too despicable.

§

The problem of evil was a part of my deconversion, but only after science had killed most of the fundamentalism.

§

This…is probably the single largest factor in pushing me from being…Christian."

§

I watched as my other BIL and best friend died a slow agonizing death from cancer at only 32 years old. I wanted to know why my prayers, my fasting and my faith were not good enough.

§

I had a major attitude change about pain and suffering in December of 1980 when a Sunday School teacher basically said (not in so many words) that John Lennon was in Hell and we should not be mourning his murder.

§

Pain and suffering are some huge problems within Christianity. Therefore were very helpful in abandoning religion.

§

There was just too much suffering. My religion couldn't give me adequate explanation as to why God allowed it.

§

How can a loving God allow his children to burn for eternity?

§

The Bible's inconsistency about human suffering and sin was a large part of what led me away from Christianity. If God created humans and God created sin and God created the world, how could God possibly not see the inevitable loss of millions or billions of humans in hell? Surely God could not make a ball and a hill and put the ball on top of that hill and be shocked when the ball rolls down. Especially Romans 9, in which Paul addresses this question and describes God as the world's most evil cosmic bully really got under my skin, and was impossible to square with pronouncements of God's love. God does not have plausible deniability for the problem of sin and evil.

§

I'm very much more existentialist in my views on suffering. No cause, no reason, pain just is. We can better ourselves by accepting that and learning from it or it can consume us. The Universe doesn't care either way. There is freedom in insignificance. My views on this changed over several years as I read existential literature and philosophy and abandoned my religious beliefs. I cannot/could not believe in a God who would punish otherwise good/just people. I could not believe in a God who saw fit to kill children, allow hurt and suffering on the scale that it exists (I work with abused/molested children, abused women, and the mentally ill). If God can't do anything about it, what good is He? If he can and chooses not to (or even MAKES IT HAPPEN), then fuck Him.

§

Recognizing the extent of the pain and suffering in the world, and the inadequacy of a God who could alleviate it, but did not, played a very big role in my deconversion process. It took several years to see it clearly.

§

Anything and everything in a universe created by an all powerful and all knowing god would logically have to the result of the intention of that god. It's illogical to think god gave us free will that wasn't entirely the result of his (male pronoun used because most religions personify god as male) intention and design. Logically, nothing that happens in a universe created by an all powerful and all knowing god can possibly be counter to his will. We live in a shared single objective reality in a materialistic, naturalistic, & macro-deterministic universe. Pain and suffering are unfortunate consequences of how the universe is playing out, and we should try to eliminate or minimize suffering whenever possible.

§

In a nutshell, I want nothing to do with a god that would allow such suffering. This played a huge part in my deconversion.

§

This was a huge contributing factor. I couldn't comprehend a God allowing so much pain.

§

This was one of the important questions that had no answers that eventually led me to atheism. I probably thought about it for a few years before realizing there was no answer.

§

This was a major part of my deconversion…The change was easy to accept, because the causes of suffering were natural (and therefore solvable) problems. I now believe we can solve all of these problems through humanistic actions.

§

When you see all those babies dying of malnutrition in Africa and all the innocents dying in wars, it makes me see a poor job that God has done. Therefore that God is unnecessary. It took about three years to deconvert, but I always wondered about even when I was a Christian.

§

I've had many people very close to me die tragically and I could no longer reconcile that fact with a loving god. Now I believe that pain and suffering are just natural occurrences and completely arbitrary.

§

I remember watching a movie about Anne Frank late in my deconversion process. At the end of the movie I said to myself "how could there possibly be a God?"

§

I read a lot of Bart Ehrmans critiques of the New Testament early on in college. I'd say his views on pain and suffering played a large role in my eventual atheist stance.

§

I always thought those views of pain and suffering were a misunderstanding of god. Then I read Job and started to question what kind of jackass this god was.

§

Probably one of the more compelling reasons that led me away from the church was why good/innocent people suffered, and why intercessory requests were randomly accepted/rejected.

§

I was told my newborn was ill due to generational sin. It took four more years for me to leave religion.

Question 38: If the inadequacy of various philosophies that seek to reconcile human suffering with the existence of a loving God (theodicy) was a contributing factor in the process of rejecting Christian faith and adopting agnosticism / atheism, how important a role did this play?

Formerly →	All Respondents Except CEF Christians N=1170	Easter-Christmas Christian, with Some Sunday Schooling N=468	Devout Liberal-Moderate Catholic N=262	Devout Conservative Catholic N=75	Devout Liberal-Moderate Protestant N=365	Devout CEF Protestant N=391
Very important	28.5%	26.1%	33.6%	25.3%	28.8%	31.2%
Somewhat important	30.4%	30.6%	28.2%	34.7%	31.0%	28.7%
Not that important	14.4%	13.7%	12.2%	13.3%	17.0%	17.9%
Not part of the process	26.7%	29.7%	26.0%	26.7%	23.3%	22.3%

Question 39: How "out" are you about your atheism / agnosticism?

Formerly →	All Respondents Except CEF Christians N=1170	Easter-Christmas Christian, with Some Sunday Schooling N=468	Devout Liberal-Moderate Catholic N=262	Devout Conservative Catholic N=75	Devout Liberal-Moderate Protestant N=365	Devout CEF Protestant N=391
Everyone knows how I feel	39.5%	42.3%	42.0%	30.7%	35.9%	34.5%
Most friends and most family know, including my parents	38.2%	39.3%	34.7%	41.3%	38.6%	38.1%
Some friends and some family know, but I have not told my parents	15.7%	13.7%	16.0%	18.7%	17.5%	19.4%
I have told very few people how I feel	6.0%	3.6%	6.9%	8.0%	7.9%	7.2%
I have told no one how I feel	0.6%	1.1%	0.4%	1.3%	0.0%	0.8%

Question 40: How emotionally difficult was the journey from Christianity to agnosticism/atheism?

Formerly →	All Respondents Except CEF Christians N=1170	Easter-Christmas Christian, with Some Sunday Schooling N=468	Devout Liberal-Moderate Catholic N=262	Devout Conservative Catholic N=75	Devout Liberal-Moderate Protestant N=365	Devout CEF Protestant N=391
Very difficult	14.4%	7.9%	13.4%	28%	20.5%	40.9%
Somewhat difficult	28.3%	24.4%	28.6%	36.0%	31.5%	30.7%
Not that difficult	31.5%	32.3%	36.3%	18.7%	29.6%	16.4%
Not difficult at all	25.9%	35.5%	21.8%	17.3%	18.4%	12.0%

Question 41: If you were to advise your former denomination (or the Christian church in general) about how to be better, how to be relevant, how to keep up with the times, what would you recommend? (Abandoning belief in a god/God is not likely; what other recommendations would you offer?)

Selected Responses[59] of Respondents Identifying as Formerly Conservative / Evangelical / Fundamentalist Protestant (366 of 391 submitted a written response):

Read and believe the Bible as allegory, myth, and figuratively. Make compassion for all people, animals, and the earth your mission.

§

I suppose, then, the best I could hope for, would be to become incrementally more tolerant, less dogmatic, and less literal about their beliefs, huh?

§

Be more tolerant.

§

Probably to not be so judgmental of those not like [them] and to not be pushy.

§

Drop the hostility to science

§

This is a very hard question. I don't know if I can make a meaningful suggestion that would not require some change in belief. Perhaps I would suggest they have a more realistic view of atheists. We're not rebelling against or angry towards a god

---

[59] Represented here are fourteen of fifty-six (14 of 56) pages submitted in the FCNA Survey. Submissions in **bold** were cited, in whole or in part, in the text of the paper. Printed here as submitted.

we don't even believe exists. When considering debating atheists or agnostics, don't waste time telling them how deep down inside atheists/agnostics really know there is a god. We REALLY do not believe.

§

Accept science a reality.

§

Be more excepting of new ideas, especially ones that are scientifically verified and don't stay tied to Bronze age dogma. Also, stop being what you vilify. It is hard to convey a message of love, friendship, forgiveness, compassion and atonement when your group is actually exhibiting these qualities the least.

§

I don't want them to be relevant and I don't want them to seemingly keeping up with times and therefore be more attractive to some people. I want them gone. I want a world free of religion. Sorry, no advice from me.

§

Keep trained, educated ministers or teachers who can converse with those of us who are intelligent, rational thinkers. Acknowledge scientific fact and societal change.

§

BE GENUINE…LOVE people. TEACH others to be compassionate and loving toward others. BE a hand and heart to the community. STOP proselytizing.

§

Mind their own business, quit pushing their beliefs on others.

§

The problem is the Bible. The battle lines are clear, and I hope they lose.

§

If Christianity was more like humanism and spent more time practicing the Golden Rule and doing what James says pure religion is, rather than being completely hung up on doctrines and creeds, it would be much better. The Christianity I was around was a system of mandatory beliefs -- either you did believe those or you weren't a true Christian.

§

Reconsider whether it's [good] to teach your children that there is a god who loves them but will send them to hell if they don't believe in him. It's not a very nice bedtime story.

§

Stop shoving God down everyone's throat, for starters. Stop assuming ex-Christians never believed at all, and were never heart-felt in their belief.

§

Abandoning dogma, encouraging critical thinking, individuality, independence and creativity. Encouraging free expression.

§

Drop the anti-gay and anti-birth control and anti-abortion advocacy.

§

Tolerance towards the homosexual community, along with other culture's and religion.

§

The Church should become inclusive. Set more chairs at the table, don't take them away. Every human being has worth, if you look for it. I left organized religion because of its constraints and condemnations. I do still have a form of Faith.

§

I would recommend reading the Bible as more of a cultural document with spiritual and metaphorical significance than literal truth. I would recommend being tolerant about the beliefs of others. And I would highly recommend not evangelizing. Christian evangelizing is terrible. It turns people off and is extremely ineffective.

§

I would tell my former Christian friends to think for themselves about what they say and do instead of just follow a book or a rhetoric or a dogma. And, most of all, consider another's feelings before you bash their thoughts and opinions.

§

Accept those who see the universe different than you are.

§

Try to read the Bible from a critical historical point of view and understand the authors' intents rather than assuming divine inspiration and inerrancy.

§

My church preached acceptance and tolerance, but they did little to act on their teachings. I suggest following Jesus's one commandment: love. Love those that are different, love those that are the same. The world would be better with a lot more love.

§

They should study current academic Biblical scholarship by the best professionals/scholars, understanding the fallible and man-made nature of the Bible and ceasing to regard it as the "word of God." They should study Christianity in light of comparative religion/mythology. They should see the symbolism in Christianity -- death to the temporary and selfish ego and life to the larger self as part of the whole -- as applicable to anyone, regardless of religion. They should keep up with science, so as not to live mentally in the Dark Ages.

§

Be more charitable.

§

Empathy, compassion for people who are not of their religion.

§

Try to be more tolerant of other religions, less certain about their own beliefs, and evaluate beliefs by their impacts for good or harm on others. Try to be less driven to impose their beliefs on others.

§

I really wouldn't have any advice. They're spreading a mind virus that, despite being what I might consider beneficial to a very select few (and usually just for a short time,) is still the cause of much needless suffering, confusion, and misinformation in the world. No version of it, however modernized, however nuanced, would I ever in good conscience wish to help carry it to another eye or ear.

§

Stop fearing. Always inquire and learn. Trust science. Stop being martyrs. Accept and tolerate those who are different and who believe differently.

§

Try to look at the world with a more nuanced view. Almost all issues are not black/white, but infinite shades.

§

Accept evolution and don't view science as an impediment to your beliefs and faith.

§

Stop the war against science, and concentrate more on the actual teachings of Jesus.

§

Stop viewing the Bible as the infallible Word of God. Use it as a reference, a history book. Not a law to which we all must be bound forever.

§

Live what you profess to believe. Love other people, even if they have beliefs that are different from your beliefs. A central tenant of Christianity is humility. Please be humble enough to consider the possibility they you may be wrong.

§

First and foremost, make your main mission one of promoting peace and justice in various particular, concrete, and legal issues. Provide help, healing, comfort, and supportive, open community for all. Conceptually: Learn to reconcile your theology's more overt legends and myths with very well-established science. Recognize and respect scriptures, traditions, and so forth AS HUMAN CREATIONS. Encourage questioning and exploring.

§

Practice what you claim to believe. Adhere directly to the teachings of Christ. To be a follower of Christ is a truly radical claim that requires an extreme approach to living and surviving.

§

To understand that the primary message of Christ was love, not hate; that the battles of faith are internal, not external; that they should read and understand Matthew 6; that they should recognize that the Bible speaks more about the corrupting nature of wealth and power than it does about homosexuality, and they should focus more on doing good and improving themselves than worrying about the inner lives of others - to be an example, in other words, rather than to force the issue.

§

Get rid of the sexist bullshit; give up on intelligent design and teach real science; start teaching that it's ok to be gay. Basically, throw out the Bible, focus on compassion and being kind to others.

§

Be more positive. Stop judging. Be understanding and compassionate. Let the focus be God and not the pastor or the show he can put on or the empire he can built.

§

Preach about the earth as a gift from god that we need to take care of. Stress the taking care of the poor, sick, needy, etc.

Emphasize how difficult it is for a rich man to enter the kingdom of heaven. Ignore many parts of the Bible.

§

I'd advise them to nurture compassion over dogma. Be more willing to tolerate differences in doctrinal details and ensure they're always subordinated to things like compassion, grace and mercy.

§

Read Kierkegaard. If I were a Christian, I'd be a Kierkegaardian. To violently do injustice to Kierkegaard and sum his thought up in a nutshell, he disregards the cognitive questions about Christianity and focuses on how to live as a Christian, which is encompassed by love for all. This means love for the homosexual, love for the girl who has an abortion, love for atheists, and etc. At no point does Kierkegaard talk about conversion or judgment, heaven or hell - he talks about acting existentially as Christ would, which seems to me the most Christ-like thing to do.

§

Do not deny science, it only make you look ignorant and when people discover the truth they are more likely to leave the church than if you had told them about it in the first place.

§

Accept science. Value evidence rather than blind faith. Admit that the Bible isn't perfect.

§

Remember to follow the Golden Rule, and keep your faith out of politics. Don't try to legislate or bully your beliefs onto others.

§

The pulpit is not the place for political messages. Focus on helping those in need, not bolstering the ego of your members.

§

Think about whether people see love, pride, or hate in your every action and word, then behave according to what you realize they'll see.

§

Behave as if He's not coming back for another 10,000 years. Take care of the Earth. It's not yours to wreck.

§

Do not convert people by your words, but by your actions.

§

Be more accepting of differences in people.

§

Spend more money on non-evangelical missions to countries and people that need it most. Don't require a conversion or bible quotes in order to help someone.

§

Abandon view of us vs. them, saved vs. lost. Love all people for what they are. Realize religion is determined by prevalent culture, not absolute truth. Examine both sides of every proposition.

§

Be more accepting, open minded, less black and white. More compassionate and caring.

§

Let science lead the way.

§

I would advise them to give up their raging homophobia!

§

Don't ignore evidence. Read. Learn all that you can about any given subject with which you disagree, then form your own opinion.

§

There is no way for the church (or the mosque or the temple) to be relevant and contemporary. It is an anachronism that yearns for a time when we were ignorant and they had power over life and death. Those days are long gone, the church is dead and we are in the process of burying the rotting corpse.

§

Forget the Old Testament entirely and focus exclusively on the teachings of Jesus.

§

If Christianity hopes to survive, they would have to follow the advice of John Shelby Spong. They would have to stop persecuting gays, persecuting non-believers, inhibiting science, and asking people to believe repugnant and ridiculous things.

§

Don't be afraid of science. **Stop watching 700 Club and Fox News.**

§

Fundamentalist evangelicals can't do much to keep up with the times as adherence to the literal word of God is so central to the denomination. This rigidity actually made it easier to get to atheism - I did not make any stops in other belief systems along the way. If the one true God wasn't real, why would any of them be?

§

Stop speaking in comfortable platitudes and theodicies when you don't understand something about the world. Don't pretend as though you know what God thinks or how He feels about this or that issue. Be honest when you don't know something, don't make excuses for God.

§

1) Don't view the bible as inerrant. Even a cursory reading shows it clearly isn't. Doing so demonstrates it's a false religion not describing a god (if it exists) of this universe. 2) Get out of politics. 3) Cut out anything that Paul wrote, and start worshiping Jesus and his teachings. Be a Jesus-Based Christian, not an old-testament-god-fearing or a Paul-based Christian.

§

Compare the lives of believers and non-believers. They aren't as different as one would think.

§

Choose humanism: love people for who they are. Respect other people. Follow the Golden Rule ("Do unto others ...") Stop being so judgmental.

§

The biggest piece of advice I could give to my former denomination would be to keep your views from controlling how others live their lives. For example, stop trying pass legislation against homosexuals, stop trying to force children in public schools to pray, basically stop ignoring the 1st Amendment.

§

Keep church and state separate.

§

Be willing to admit you don't have all the answers... 2. Stop opposing loving, committed relationships just because they fall outside of your accepted norms.

§

To encourage doing rather than (or in conjunction with) prayer.

§

Admitting uncertainty and fallibility in one's interpretation of the Bible is essential in alleviating the tension between different religions, different branches within each religion, even different individuals within a given congregation.

§

Live the teachings of Jesus (care for the poor, the sick, the disadvantaged, do not judge, note that he never said anything about homosexuality), not the perversions of his teachings that flourish today America. (I often see postings on Facebook about "Republican Jesus" -- that's pretty close to the Jesus I grew up hearing about, and he's very different than the Jesus in the Bible. Fixing that dissonance would at least remove some of the hypocrisy that is rampant in fundamentalist Christianity.

§

If the church kept their noses out of everyone's business, they would have a lot fewer enemies. Telling people about Jesus doesn't mean that you have to try to force people to live their lives like you do. Offer the good news, but accept that people have the right to make their own choices. Practice your Christianity, I have no problem with that, but don't try to impose your rules on others. I am for equality for all in this country, and that includes Christians, as long as you don't step on anyone else's equality.

§

Use your brain. Use common sense. Do some research. Don't be so naive and just blindly believe what you read in the bible.

§

Read the Bible as you would any other book, from start to finish and think about what it says... Not what you were told it says.

§

Let the mystery be.

§

Stop being so hateful. Stop being so concerned with politics. Go out in the city/world and honestly help people who need it. Not sermons, but food and water, an ear for their problems and concerns, a roof over their head. Real, honest help.

§

Stop being dicks to everyone with a different opinion.

§

Fear based teachings should have less of a place in modern society.

§

Remember humility and compassion and brotherly love. None of us is so great we cannot fall. And almost all who

have fallen can be redeemed, if not by religion, then by common human grace. Forgive the past. Enjoy the present. Hope for the future. Judge sparingly, forgive often, and love always.

§

Read the whole bible. Read science. Does the biblical god appear moral to you?

§

Listen to scientists. Listen to the pain other people experience without trying to fix them or save them. Help other people out of the goodness of your heart and not to win some reward or to please some god. Know that atheists are not immoral bastards. Know that if you were another religion, you wouldn't want people to trample on your rights, so stop trampling on other people.

§

Accept science, don't be dogmatic.

§

Be good for humanities sake, not because of fear.

§

Abandon any opposition or ambivalence to science, and drop all pretention of superiority over those of different racial, sexual, or political orientation.

§

Live and let live.

§

Don't tear your people down telling them how horrible they are just so you can "build them back up again". It's abusive.

§

If you find yourselves agreeing with the GOP, you're on the wrong track.

§

Heed the Sermon on the Mount more than Deuteronomy; loving thy neighbor is far better witness than pointing out the note in your brother's eye.

§

Stop hating each other.

§

I really don't see how churches can be any more relevant than Santa Claus or the Tooth Fairy. Honestly, I think Harry Potter or Lord of the Rings has more to teach us than the Bible.

§

Lighten up, get out of politics, get out of judgment.

§

I would ask them to focus on the positive aspects of Christ's message, and not on the divisive parts. The emphasis on homosexuality in particular is really disturbing in modern Protestantism.

§

To keep the focus not on scripture, dogma, or sin, but to focus on providing loving care and comfort to those in need in the community. To be a place where the downtrodden can lay their heads. Arguments over theology are a waste of time when there are people in the community starving and sleeping in the streets.

§

Give up on the gay thing. Give up on abortion. These issues only divide people, and are hurting the overall perception of the American church. Be more like Christ, and less like Jerry Falwell.

§

Show some humility in your beliefs. There are countless people that can read the same Bible and come to different views, so everyone should hold their doctrines loosely.

§

Focus more on doing acts of service instead of condemning people or restricting people's rights, such as opposing gay marriage.

§

Don't attempt to convert your religious views into law and compel everyone to comply (like Prop 8 in CA)

§

The power of self-righteousness is very similar to the power of "the dark side" in Star Wars. It's seductive and easy to access, but the payoff is that you train yourself to be a sociopath. Watch yourself closely and pay attention to what you really believe.

§

Understand the scientific method and study evolution. Get to know non-believers.

§

Don't assume that God is a Republican. Don't mix nationalism with religion (my church had a big annual 4th of July celebration that turned me off). Accept gay rights.

Bibliography

Books

Aronson, Ronald. *Living Without God: New Directions for Atheists, Agnostics, Secularists, and the Undecided.* Berkeley, CA: Counterpoint, 2008. Print.

Babinski, Edward T. *Leaving the Fold: Testimonies of Former Fundamentalists.* Amherst, NY: Prometheus Books, 2003. Print.

Barker, Dan. *Godless: How an Evangelical Preacher Became One of America's Leading Atheists.* Berkeley, CA: Ulysses Press, 2008. Print.

Blackford, Russell and Udo Schüklenk, eds. 50 *Voices of Disbelief: Why We Are Atheists.* West Sussex, UK: Blackwell Publishing, 2009. Print.

Borg, Marcus J. *Meeting Jesus Again for the First Time: The Historical Jesus and the Heart of Contemporary Faith.* New York: HarperSanFrancisco, 1994. Print.

Brogaard, Betty. *The Homemade Atheist: A Former Evangelical Woman's Freethought Journey to Happiness.* Berkeley, CA: Ulysses Press, 2010. Print.

Cox, Harvey. *The Future of Faith.* New York: HarperCollins, 2009. Print.

---. *The Secular City: A Celebration of its Liberties and an Invitation to its Disciplines.* New York: The Macmillan Company, 1965. Print.

Dawkins, Richard. *The God Delusion.* New York: Houghton Mifflin, 2006. Print.

Dennett, Daniel C. *Breaking the Spell: Religion as a Natural*

Phenomenon. New York: Viking, 2006. Print.

Eagleton, Terry. *Reason, Faith, and Revolution: Reflections on the God Debate*. New Haven: Yale University Press, 2009. Print.

Ehrman, Bart D. *God's Problem: How the Bible Fails to Answer Our Most Important Question—Why We Suffer*. New York: HarperCollins, 2008. Print.

---. *Misquoting Jesus: The Story Behind Who Changed the Bible and Why*. San Francisco: HarperSanFrancisco, 2005. Print.

Everett, Daniel. *Don't Sleep, There are Snakes: Life and Language in the Amazonian Jungle*. New York: Vintage Books, 2008. Print.

Gardner, Martin. *The Flight of Peter Fromm*. 1973. Amherst, NY: Prometheus Books, 1994. Print.

Hahn, Scott, and Benjamin Wiker. *Answering the New Atheism: Dismantling Dawkins' Case Against God*. Steubenville, OH: Emmaus Road Publishing, 2008. Print.

Harris, Sam. *Letter to a Christian Nation*. New York: Alfred A. Knopf, 2006. Print.

---. *The End of Faith: Religion, Terror, and the Future of Reason*. New York: W.W. Norton, 2004. Print.

Hart, David Bentley. *Atheist Delusions: The Christian Revolution and Its Fashionable Enemies*. New Haven: Yale University Press, 2009. Print.

Hedges, Chris. *American Fascists: The Christian Right and the War on America*. New York: Free Press, 2006. Print.

---. *When Atheism Becomes Religion: America's New*

Fundamentalists. New York: Free Press, 2008. Print.

Hempton, David. *Evangelical Disenchantment: Nine Portraits of Faith and Doubt*. New Haven: Yale University Press, 2008. Print.

Hitchcock, S.C. *Disbelief 101: A Young Person's Guide to Atheism*. Tucson, AZ: See Sharp Press, 2009. Print.

Hitchens, Christopher. *God is Not Great: How Religion Poisons Everything*. New York: Twelve, 2007. Print.

Kushner, Harold S. *When Bad Things Happen to Good People*. New York: Avon Books, 1981. Print.

Lepp, Ignace. *Atheism in Our Time: A Psychoanalyst's Dissection of the Modern Varieties of Unbelief*. New York: The Macmillan Company, 1963. Print.

Lobdell, William. *Losing My Religion: How I Lost My Faith Reporting on Religion in America—and Found Unexpected Peace*. New York: Collins, 2009. Print.

Loftus, John W, ed. *The Christian Delusion: Why Faith Fails*. Amherst, NY: Prometheus Books, 2010. Print.

---. *Why I Became an Atheist: A Former Preacher Rejects Christianity*. Amherst, NY: Prometheus Books, 2008. Print.

Mark, Jeffrey. *Christian No More: A Personal Journey of Leaving Christianity and How You Can Leave Too*. Cincinnati: Reasonable Press, 2008. Print.

Marsden, George M. *Fundamentalism and American Culture*. 2nd ed. Oxford: Oxford University Press, 2006. Print.

Masterson, Patrick. *Atheism and Alienation: A Study of the Philosophical Sources of Contemporary Atheism*. Notre

Dame, IN: University of Notre Dame Press, 1971. Print.

McGrath, Alister. *The Twilight of Atheism: The Rise and Fall of Disbelief in the Modern World*. New York: Doubleday, 2004. Print.

Onfray, Michel. *Atheist Manifesto: The Case Against Christianity, Judaism, and Islam*. New York: Arcade Publishing, 2005. Print.

Paulos, John Allen. *Irreligion: A Mathematician Explains Why the Arguments for God Just Don't Add Up*. New York: Hill and Wang, 2008. Print.

Smith, George H. *Why Atheism?* Amherst, NY: Prometheus Books, 2000. Print.

Templeton, Charles. *Farewell to God: My Reasons for Rejecting the Christian Faith*. Toronto, ON: McClelland & Stewart, 1996. Print.

The Bible. Chicago, IL: Consolidated Book Publishers, 1947. Print. Authorized King James Version.

Thrower, James. *Western Atheism: A Short History*. Amherst, NY: Prometheus Press, 2000. Print.

Tocqueville, Alexis de. *Democracy in America*. Vol. 2. 1840. Trans. Henry Reeve. New York: Vintage Books, 1945. Print.

Westphal, Merold. *Suspicion and Faith: The Religious Uses of Modern Atheism*. New York: Fordham University Press, 1998. Print.

Articles/Essays

Baggini, Julian. "Atheism in America: Why Won't the U.S. Accept Its Atheists?" *Slate Magazine.com*. Slate Magazine. Web. 5 February 2012.

Bascom, John. "Atheism in Colleges." *The North American Review* 132 (January 1881): 32-40. Print.

Bingham, Larry. "'Hateful Christians' vs. 'Kind Atheists.'" *The Oregonian*. 5 April 2012. Web. 10 April 2012.

Berry, Robby. "How I Became an Ex-Christian." *Infidels.org*. n.d. Web. 20 August 2008.

---. "Why Come Out as an Atheist." *Infidels.org*. n.d. Web. 20 August 2009.

Brennan, Emily. "The Unbelievers." *NYTimes.com*. New York Times, 29 August 2011. Web. 25 November 2011.

Briggs, Carolyn S. "Waiting for Lightning to Strike: A Wobbly Agnostic among the Atheists." *Religion Dispatches.org*. Religion Dispatches. 18 October 2011. Web. 7 February 2012.

Bultmann, Rudolf. "Protestant Theology and Atheism." *The Journal of Religion* 52.4 (October 1972): 331-335. Print.

Campbell, David E. and Robert D. Putnam. "God and Caesar in America: Why Mixing Religion and Politics is Bad for Both." *Foreign Affairs* March/April 2012: 34-43. Print

Dyck, Drew. "The Leavers: More than in Previous Generations, 20- and 30-somethings are Abandoning the Faith. Why?" *Christianity Today* November 2010: 40-44. Print.

Edgell, Penny, Joseph Gerteis, and Douglas Hartmann. "Atheists as 'Other': Moral Boundaries and Cultural Membership in American Society." *American Sociological Review* 71 (April 2006): 211-234. Print.

Galen, Luke W. "Profiles of the Godless: Results from a

Survey of the Nonreligious." *Free Inquiry* (Aug.-Sep. 2009): 41-45. Print.

Goodstein, Laurie. "More Atheists Shout It From the Rooftops." *New York Times* 27 April 2009. A1. Print.

Hout, Michael and Claude S. Fischer. "Why More Americans Have No Religious Preference: Politics and Generations." *American Sociological Review* 67 (April 2002): 165-190. Print.

Kosmin, Barry A., and Ariela Keysar. "American Religious Identification Survey." *AmericanReligiousSurvey-ARIS.org*. March 2009. Web. 22 May 2011.

Ingersoll, Robert Green. "About the Holy Bible" (1894). Infidels.org. Web. 5 December 2011.

"Jefferson's Letter to the Danbury Baptists." *LOC.gov*. Library of Congress. Web. 15 February 2012.

Lebo, Lauri. "The Social Cost of Atheism." *ReligionDispatches.com*. Religion Dispatches. 10 June 2010. Web. 10 June 2010.

Lee, Lois, and Stephen Bullivant. "Where do Atheists Come From?" *NewScientist.com*. New Scientist. March 2010. Web. 4 March 2010.

Lugo, Luis. "U.S. Religious Knowledge Survey." *PewForum.org*. Pew Forum on Religion & Public Life. September 2010. Web. 22 May 2011.

MacDonald, G. Jeffrey. "Atheists Choose 'De-Baptism' to Renounce Childhood Faith." *USAToday.com*. USA Today, July 22, 2009. Web. 15 March 2010.

Maritain, Jacques. "On the Meaning of Contemporary Atheism." *The Review of Politics* 11 (July 1949): 267-

280. Print.

Phillips, Michael M. "A Chaplain and an Atheist Go to War." *WSJ.com*. The Wall Street Journal, 4 September 2010. Web. 2 October 2010.

Shaffer, Ryan. "The *Humanist* Interview with Leo Behe." *TheHumanist.org*. The Humanist, September/October 2011. Web. 28 August 2011.

Spiegel, Jim. "Unreasonable Doubt: The Reasons for Unbelief are More Complex than Many Atheists Let On." *ChristianityToday.com*. Christianity Today January 2011. Web. 22 May 2011.

Steinfels, Peter. "Looking to Other Religions, and to Atheism, for Clarity in Faith." *NYTTimes.com*. New York Times, 7 November 2009. Web. 9 November 2009.

"Support for Same-Sex Marriage Edges Upward." *PeoplePress.org*. People Press, 6 October 2010. Web. 13 October 2010.

"U.S. Religious Knowledge Survey." *PewResearch.org*. Pew Forum on Religion & Public Life, September 2010. Web. 5 March 2011.

Walsh, Steve. "New Atheist Movie 'The Ledge' Evangelizes Godlessness." *CNN.com*. Cable News Network, 8 July 2011. Web. 4 October 2011.

Wilder, Charly. "I Don't Believe in Atheists." *Salon.com*. Salon, 18 August 2009. Web. 22 May 2011.

About the Author

The author holds a bachelor's degree in secondary social studies education from Southeast Missouri State University, Cape Girardeau; a master's degree in history from the University of Missouri at St. Louis; and a master's degree in religion from Harvard University Extension School in Cambridge, Massachusetts. He was baptized in the Southern Baptist denomination at age 10 and re-baptized with the Assemblies of God at 16, where he served as president of his congregation's youth group, Christ's Ambassadors, and wholeheartedly embraced a fundamentalist and apocalyptic brand of conservative American Christianity. He no longer does. He currently tutors and teaches American history, political science, and comparative religion at a community college in southeast Missouri. He may be contacted at rodneycwilsonbooks@yahoo.com.

Printed in Great Britain
by Amazon